Special Interests in Art Therapy with Autistic People

of related interest

Art Therapy with Adults with Autism Spectrum Disorder
Beth Gonzalez-Dolginko
ISBN 978 1 78592 831 4
eISBN 978 1 78450 972 9

Art as an Early Intervention Tool for Children with Autism
Nicole Martin
ISBN 978 1 84905 807 0
eISBN 978 1 84642 956 9

The Amazing Autistic Brain Cards
150 Cards with Strengths and Challenges for Positive Autism Discussions
Glòria Durà-Vilà
Illustrated by Rebecca Tatternorth
ISBN 978 1 78775 430 0

The Handbook of Art Therapy and Digital Technology
Cathy Malchiodi, PhD
Foreword by Dr Val Huet
ISBN 978 1 78592 792 8
eISBN 978 1 78450 774 9

SPECIAL INTERESTS in ART THERAPY with AUTISTIC PEOPLE

A Neurodiversity-Positive Approach to Empower and Engage Participants

JESSICA WOOLHISER STALLINGS

Jessica Kingsley Publishers
London and Philadelphia

First published in Great Britain in 2022 by Jessica Kingsley Publishers
An imprint of Hodder & Stoughton Ltd
An Hachette Company

1

Front cover image source: Vectorstock®. The cover image is for illustrative purposes only, and any person featuring is a model.

A CIP catalogue record for this title is available from the British Library and the Library of Congress

ISBN 978 1 78775 908 4
eISBN 978 1 78775 909 1

Printed and bound in the United States by Integrated Books International

Jessica Kingsley Publishers' policy is to use papers that are natural, renewable and recyclable products and made from wood grown in sustainable forests. The logging and manufacturing processes are expected to conform to the environmental regulations of the country of origin.

Jessica Kingsley Publishers
Carmelite House
50 Victoria Embankment
London EC4Y 0DZ

www.jkp.com

Contents

Acknowledgements

Thank you to Lynn Kapitan, Chris Belkofer, Penny Orr, Máire Johnson, Bruce Moon, and Alex Kapitan for your guidance and help in developing the research on which this book is based. Thank you to my friends Libby, Gaelynn, Trina, Huma, Kai, Melanie, and Tzafi. Without your friendship and support, this book wouldn't have happened. Thank you to my parents Jim and Debbie, in-laws Fran and Gordon, and brother Josh for your loving support. Thank you to my love Ben, for your seemingly endless love and support. Thank you for being my cheerleader and for grounding me.

Thank you most of all to my neurodivergent and autistic clients, friends, and consultants who have taught me so much. Thank you most of all to Dani, Amber, Klyde, and RJ!

A NOTE ABOUT LANGUAGE

In this book I use both identity-first (autistic person) and person-first language (person with autism) as there is no current consensus on which is most appropriate.

Part One

CHAPTER I

Why This Book?

INTRODUCTION

> Those who work with autistics on a more empathic level realize that perseveration is not simply mindless repetition without significance. What is said, drawn, sung or written often holds the key to the child's salient concerns. One only need listen seriously and see in order to partake of their struggles. (Henley 1989, p.53)

Nearly 20 years of clinical work, first as a behavioral therapy technician and currently as a professional art therapist and mental health counselor with individuals with autism, led me to explore these so-called "perseverations" or special interests and their potential role in art therapy. Throughout this time, it became apparent to me that popular culture cues were key to building relationships with autistic children and adults. My first experience was with a preschooler who loved *Veggie Tales*, an American children's show featuring animated vegetable characters. This child used household items like toothpaste and toothbrushes to act out their favorite of "Silly Songs with Larry"—"His Cheeseburger"—in the bathroom throughout the day. Such special interests or "perseverations" consist of intense fixation on something—such as "His Cheeseburger" or a video game. These occur for many reasons, which may include, but are not limited to, coping with anxiety or dealing with over- or under-stimulation with sensory input (Boyd *et al.* 2007). In this child's case, the interest provided me a window into their world, a way to build our relationship, leading to me singing along and using *Veggie Tales* as a way to capture and hold the child's attention.

It is important for me to note here that my early work with folks with autism was as a provider of applied behavior analysis (ABA) and running a social skills training program, and I am likely at fault for damage caused by such approaches. I have observed firsthand some of the problems of these approaches and worked to learn from folks with autism. The specific concerns with such approaches will be described in Chapters 2 and 3. My hope now is to use my position as an expert in the art therapy field to educate others of the problems with these approaches, and I do this in part through teaching classes and training other clinicians. As a non-autistic clinician, I am always learning how to be a better clinician for my autistic therapy participants, and remain engaged in consultation with my participants with autism and in pursuing resources to help myself be better informed and more sensitive.

In my current work, I leverage these special interests to build rapport and to help identify and address treatment goals. In my experience, these interests are often derived from popular culture consumption. For the purposes of this book, popular culture refers to anything derived from entertainment media such as television, YouTube, video games, books, comics/graphic novels, sports, toys, and other interests consumed frequently in the United States (and possibly beyond). In some areas, popular culture may include large churches and other spiritual subjects or objects. It is worth noting that everyone has special interests—a sports team, superheroes, anime, pets—although perseverations are cited as a symptom of autism because the intensity of autistic people's interests is often higher than that of non-autistic folks; simply having special interests is a general human characteristic. In the pages of this book you will find information on the benefits and drawbacks of these special interests, as well as guidelines for how to work with these interests in an art therapy setting. Additionally, this book provides an overview of common approaches to therapy with autistic participants, problems with those approaches, and descriptions of autism positive approaches. The book culminates in Part Two in a framework for an autism positive approach to art therapy based on popular culture special interests.

CONNECTING WITH OUR ART THERAPY PARTICIPANTS

In my experience, imagery from popular culture is unavoidable when working with individuals on the autism spectrum. In fact, popular culture can be the most accessible way to build relationships and foster communication between those who are *neurotypical* (those whose neurocognitive functioning is considered typical; see Attwood 1998) and those who are *neurodivergent* (those whose neurocognitive functioning is considered atypical; see Silberman 2015; Walker 2021). The term *neurodiversity* refers to "the diversity of human minds, the infinite variation in neurocognitive functioning within our species" (Walker 2021, para. 8). Advocates for the neurodiversity paradigm argue that the ways people with conditions such as autism and dyslexia interact with the world are not wrong but rather just different from how neurotypical people interact with the world (Ne'eman 2012; Robison 2013; Walker 2021).

When I began working with individuals with autism in 2001, I witnessed and later explicitly encouraged interaction through popular culture imagery and play. I had long suspected that the many conversations I'd had with neurodivergent participants about professional wrestling, *Dragon Ball Z* (a Japanese anime TV series), "Five Nights at Freddy's" (a video game), *Doctor Who* (a British science fiction TV series), Disney everything, and so on were integral to therapeutic relationships. As a young clinician I saw value in using my firsthand understanding of some of these topics and my curiosity about others in building relationships with my preteen and adolescent participants diagnosed with autism, Asperger syndrome, and pervasive developmental disorder (all diagnoses now under the autism spectrum disorder umbrella). However, I often felt guilty about engaging in these subjects during therapy sessions as I worried that others would judge them as a waste of time at worst, or tangential and off-topic at best. I spent time looking for and printing out images from online searches on these subjects to encourage my participants to engage in the art process and to spark interest in understanding that we all have likes and dislikes, some of which are shared and some of which are different. It helped that I was initially working in a recreation therapy department that required a "leisure education" component, so I could make the case that these subjects related to my participants' leisure preferences and helped them understand the preferences of other group members.

When I left that job to become an academic in higher education, I took these lessons with me. I created and implemented a pro bono art therapy social group for teens with autism. Quickly we focused on anime and Disney. When I started working in private practice, I immediately noticed that inviting discussion of YouTube or even watching some of the videos together encouraged my participants, who were at times as young as seven, to interact with me and to warm up to art making. Yet I still wondered if I was being frivolous or letting them down in some way.

My doctoral studies encouraged me to reexamine these concerns and to view these interactions in a different light, in consideration of the autonomy and emancipatory self-determination of my participants in these interactions, and in seeing these interactions as the bridge between neurotypical and neurodivergent worlds. I have grown to respect how my participants have taught me through these interactions about themselves and how they see the world, as well as how these interactions have helped me partner with my participants as they navigate the neurotypical world. These interests provide powerful metaphors, means of connection, and ways to cope with anxiety, as demonstrated in the following, which are some examples from my practice:

- An adolescent participant took on the persona of a video game character and used this identity as a shield against bullying and social anxiety. Rather than speaking of themself directly, they utilized characters from the game to engage in social skills practice and to work through other issues they needed to address.

- A preadolescent participant who was nonverbal communicated her feelings by humming Disney songs—in particular, "Someday my prince will come"—when they did not want to do something.
- An adolescent boy with co-occurring selective mutism would only interact with me through the use of Avengers-themed LEGO® bricks.
- An eight-year-old client would only address his anxieties through the personas of "Five Nights at Freddy's" characters; attempting to address them in other ways only increased his anxiety.
- Two siblings, eight and nine years old, together worked through their anxieties about an abusive home and absent father through a *Star Wars* sticker collage.
- A 10-year-old boy played out violent fantasies based on video games and their own trauma history through LEGO® bricks, and could eventually identify the "criminals" as their parent and at times themself. Their play poignantly displayed the security they felt with their adoptive mother through the character of the criminal's mother who gave the criminal unconditional love in spite of what they had done.
- An adolescent client had an obsession with the Christian end of days, often referred to as "the rapture" (as heavily emphasized by their church and also in the popular Left Behind book series), providing many learning opportunities in regard to social appropriateness and friendship.

- A participant related to the alien character Oh from the 2015 film *Home* as a personal symbol, acknowledging that Oh's awkwardness and social difficulties were much like their own social difficulties.
- An adolescent participant dealt with the loss of their step-parent to a chronic illness and the prospect that their sibling would also die from the same illness by creating art and stories based on a video game about a nuclear apocalypse (in which a character died of cancer). When asked, they stated that the game reminded them of how they might outlive their sibling.

I can think of countless other examples that involved popular culture references and media, such as *Thomas the Tank Engine*, the film *Cheaper by the Dozen*, various Disney movies, singer Adam Levine, and even professional wrestling. Although all children play and it is not uncommon for neurotypical children to repeat their imaginary play adventures over and over, the difference for autistic children is that they often do not invite others to interact in their imaginary play or to come into their imaginary worlds. Whereas neurotypical children reach out on their own for social connection, an autistic child often does not, or at least not in a way that is identifiable to a neurotypical person. Despite the lack of or atypicality of social initiation, however, these interests do represent a means of connection. Clinicians can show interest in these interests, allowing them to meet participants where they are, and encouraging joint attention to help build rapport and social relationships. By doing so, they can meet autistic participants on their own terms rather than attempting to get them to conform to a neurotypical agenda.

Additionally, I find that the expectation of creating original imagery in art therapy creates a challenge for autistic children. Based on conversations I have had with peers and other professionals, a preference for popular culture imagery—so common among people with autism—is viewed by some as evidence of a paucity or lack of imagination. For many art therapists and the general public, imagination is equated with an ability to create completely original content or imagery; however, with the advent of the internet it is increasingly clear that many people (with and without autism) express their imaginations through derivative works such as memes, fan fiction (Burt 2017), and other popular culture responses. In my own experience with autistic folks, popular culture interests and references expand imagination, promote creativity, and increase metaphorical understanding and communication in a similar way as fan fiction. Popular culture figures often provide an avatar for the participant to explore and build communication, self-regulation, and other skills. I would be remiss to not mention that an autistic child's selection of popular cultural interests and figures may also represent their desire to connect with others over media with which many people are already familiar. Collectively, these interests provide a way to relate to and communicate with others, which art therapists may use to build therapeutic relationships and facilitate therapeutic goals.

ADDITIONAL EVIDENCE TO MAKE THESE CONNECTIONS

My clinical observations are supported by the book (Suskind 2014) and documentary (Williams 2016) entitled *Life, Animated: A Story of Sidekicks, Heroes, and Autism* that is based on a true story. The family of a young man diagnosed with autism, Owen Suskind, discovered that he was communicating with them through what appeared to be non-purposeful repetition of words or phrases (known as echolalia) that Owen heard from Disney movies—the animated character Iago from *Aladdin* in particular. Upon this realization, the family joined Owen in watching these movies repeatedly and speaking the dialogue to each other, eventually helping Owen to learn and utilize language independent of the echolalia. Owen's family integrated his special interests into his schooling and therapies, and Owen thrived. After Owen's father consulted with his son's psychiatrist, he theorized that Owen's mimicking of these characters compensated for his impaired inner speech (Suskind 2014). Owen's echolalia and subsequent elaborations of what his favorite Disney characters might say allowed him to better process events and see them from different perspectives, in a way that he was unable to do without the characters.

Although this is just one case, in the context of my nearly 20 years of experience working with autistic individuals, Owen Suskind's story affirms and provides further evidence of the importance of popular culture references in treatment and everyday life. Engagement in the individual's special interests is a strategy, as seen in the example of Owen, of bridging worlds to access social relationships and build understanding. Furthermore, it emphasizes the necessity of art therapists truly meeting participants where they are, understanding their different neurological needs, and working within the communication channels their participants offer.

These observations are also supported in Henley's 1989 case study regarding Nadia Chomyn, a well-known autistic artist, and in his memoir about working with neurodivergent individuals (Henley 2018). He utilized Chomyn's interest in print catalogs to build rapport with her and later to build rapport with other participants through listening to their interests in anime and video games while praising their art products based on these interests (Henley 2018). As a pioneering art therapist with autistic people, Henley supported the use of special interests in treatment, recognizing that they were often related to popular culture and could be used to build rapport and encourage participation in art therapy.

Nadia Chomyn's was a case that was originally made famous by the researcher Selfe (1977). Selfe conducted a three-year longitudinal study of Chomyn beginning when she was three years old and diagnosed with autism and severe mental retardation. Chomyn was also an "artistic savant" who had developed an adult-like artistic style and drew horses repeatedly, as well as other farm animals, seemingly inspired by her favorite storybook. Her artistic ability surfaced while her mother was ill and later regressed after her mother's death.

Henley (1989) worked with Chomyn as an adult with the goal of reinforcing her previous interest in art and to see if her artistic ability would resurface. Henley theorized that Chomyn had utilized art to self-soothe during her mother's illness, and suggested that the art and materials served as a sort of transitional object for her.

Henley (1989) worked with the nearly 30-year-old Chomyn in her home. He reported that she initially appeared upset by his presence; however, after he sat in her house for a time she grew excited, speaking in echolalia about her contemporary special interests, which Henley described as the Sears catalog and saw as her attempt to communicate. With this realization, he engaged with Chomyn by encouraging her to show him her catalogs. The next day, Henley continued with the joint catalog viewing. After a short period, he provided Chomyn with paper and black felt tip pens. Because she initially grew agitated when her father, who was present, also encouraged her to draw, Henley asked her father to leave. Henley sat across the room from Chomyn as she explored the materials and scribbled. He slowly moved closer until she tolerated him sitting at the table with her. She then became increasingly engaged in the art making, initially filling paper with scribbles, but working up to making representative images. Over subsequent days, Henley showed her the storybook she had been inspired by as a young child and her previous drawings, and encouraged her to replicate them. She did so, and although her artistic style was not as mature as it had once been, she was able to create pseudo-naturalistic images.

Henley (1989) noted that Chomyn had engaged in extensive cognitive and behavioral therapies after the death of her mother, and theorized that this treatment may actually have facilitated her artistic regression because it "fail[ed] to support her during a time of personal crisis" (p.52). He postulated that if Chomyn had been provided with art therapy, this may have helped better facilitate her development, both affectively and cognitively. Henley observed that in this case and others like it, "the process of making art should be seen not simply as an elaborate symptom as but as an adaptive, positive means of self-expression that has value as a conduit toward both creative and mental growth" (1989, p.55). He conjectured that art therapists can tap into these special interests to provide interventions that are minimally invasive.

WHY ART THERAPY? WHY THIS BOOK?

At the time of this publication there is little exploration of the use of special interests to build therapeutic relationships with autistic participants. Popular culture and other special interests, which can appear to the uninformed witness as senseless fascinations, provide an opening for communication and relationship building. Engagement with participants in this way acknowledges that autism is a different way of thinking and interacting with the world and not an illness to be cured (Silberman 2015), encouraging an autism positive approach to art therapy.

By its nature, art therapy places importance on metaphor and visual communication, which makes it well suited to working with autistic participants. Neuroscientists Kana, Keller, Cherkassky, Minshew, and Just (2006) found that neurological connections in the occipital lobe were thicker in autistic individuals than in research participants without autism diagnoses, indicating heavy use of visual systems in the formers' brains. Additionally, Grandin and Panek (2013) observed that autistic individuals tend to be visual, patterned, or word-fact thinkers, basing this supposition on Grandin's personal experience with autism and in experiences with other autistic people. Further support exists in cognitive psychology research, particularly the work of Kozhevnikov (2007; Blazhenkova & Kozhevnikov 2009; Kozhevnikov, Kosslyn, & Shephard 2005). Kozhevnikov's research findings essentially supported varied cognitive styles beyond the established verbal/visual binary, and therefore lend support to styles such as pattern-based thinking. The compatibility of visual and pattern thinking with the same properties in art therapy provide an argument for art therapy with autistic participants. It is necessary to reexamine common assumptions about the characteristics of individuals with autism, the effectiveness of existing therapies, and strategies for therapeutic alliance formation with these individuals in order to build a successful art therapy framework.

CONCLUSION

Art therapy is uniquely suited for many individuals with autism due to its visual nature and its ability to help individuals explore their special interests in ways that acknowledge their deeper identifications with these interests and how those connect them to the outside world. Thus far, art therapy literature acknowledges the former but not the latter, which means that it is possible that art therapists are missing opportunities to connect with participants with autism, and new clinicians are not trained to work in more effective ways. Potash (2009) asserted that traditionally in art therapy, stereotypical or popular imagery has been viewed as evidence of a lack of imagination or psychic defense; however, in the case of individuals with autism, these images are truly personal communications. In the upcoming pages, this book will examine the history of autism treatment, the role of art therapy, neurodivergence and self-advocacy, and explore how integration of special interests provides a powerful tool for both art therapists and participants with autism in building relationships and centering emotional needs.

CHAPTER 2

An Autism Positive Approach

Understanding Autism and Neurodivergence

To develop an art therapy treatment framework for individuals on the autism spectrum, it is important to understand the core characteristics of autism and the challenges that these individuals may face. I will illustrate these characteristics and challenges through a description of the diagnostic criteria as detailed in the fifth edition of the *Diagnostic and statistical manual of mental disorders* (DSM-5; APA 2013), often targeted symptoms, and the constructs of the neurodiversity paradigm and autism positive approaches. Each of these aspects is explored in the following section.

AUTISM SPECTRUM DISORDER DIAGNOSIS

The DSM-5 classifies autism spectrum disorder with two primary areas of impairment and/or behavioral excesses: (a) deficits in social communication and interaction and emotional understanding (social cognition); and (b) restricted repetitive behaviors (RRBs), including perseverative interests, repetitive motor behavior/self-stimulatory behavior (commonly known as *stimming*), difficulty with transitions and/or breaks in routine, and sensory under- or over-stimulation. To receive a diagnosis of autism, these traits must be present in early childhood but may become more severe with age. Individuals must also experience difficulties in social, occupational, and/or daily living activities at clinically significant levels. For specific wording of these criteria please consult the DSM-5 (APA 2013, p.50).

Autism has several specifiers associated with the diagnosis, and of primary import are the three levels of severity. Level 1, "requiring support," is the mildest, marked primarily by deficits in social interaction and initiation along with some RRBs; this level encompasses individuals previously diagnosed with Asperger syndrome under the fourth edition of the DSM (DSM-IV). Level 2, "requiring substantial support," includes additional impairments in verbal and nonverbal communication and more severe RRBs. Level 3, "requiring very substantial support," features more substantial difficulties in verbal and nonverbal communication. These individuals are often nonverbal or minimally verbal, experience difficulty with transitions, and exhibit various RRBs (APA 2013).

NEURODIVERGENCE

Historically autism and other neurological diagnoses were regarded as impairments stemming from inadequate parenting, neglect/abuse, and childhood schizophrenia, among other stigmatizing beliefs, resulting in institutionalization. However, more recently autism and other neurological disorders (including attention deficit hyperactivity disorder, ADHD) are now considered part of a range of "normal, natural variations in the human genome" (Robison 2013, para. 1). Some consider these different styles of neurocognitive functioning to be "dysfunctions" only in comparison to neurotypical individuals. *Neurotypical*, a term coined by Attwood (1998), initially referred to individuals without autism but has now broadened to refer to individuals without diagnosed neurological conditions or whose neurocognitive functioning is considered typical and accepted in society at large (Liebowitz 2016; Silberman 2015).

A group of autistic adults founded the Autistic Self Advocacy

Network (ASAN) in 2006 in response to a lack of engagement of neurotypical scientists with autistic adults in the dialogue regarding autism and its treatment (ASAN 2017). This group identifies with the larger disability rights movement that advocates for equal access and accommodation for individuals with a wide range of disabilities. ASAN adopted the term *neurodiversity* to engage a broader discussion of autism treatment that had previously focused specifically on finding a cure. It engages individuals with a variety of diagnoses (although primarily autism) in self-advocacy for independence and accommodation rather than focusing on a cure (ASAN 2017; Ne'eman 2012). Neurodiversity movement advocates have embraced the language of the disability rights movement and its statement "nothing about us without us" (ASAN 2015, 2017; Silberman 2015). This refers to the desire of all people to make independent decisions and to have physical and psychological autonomy or self-determination, regardless of disability (Charlton 1998), and it has taken on the same meaning in the neurodiversity movement (Silberman 2015).

Therapists are challenged to understand the concerns of ASAN and the neurodiversity movement and avoid imposing one-size-fits-all treatments or treating aspects of autism that do not need treatment, such as an obsession with Pokémon that does not interfere with daily functioning. Alternatively, if said obsession does interfere but can be worked with, then the obsession does not need to be eliminated (a fact that will also have a bearing on treatment). Proponents of the neurodiversity paradigm argue that individuals with autism do not need a cure; rather, they need adaptations to help them optimally function in the neurotypical world (Liebowitz 2016; Silberman 2015).

ASAN (2017) advocates for acceptance of neurodiversity and promotion of the stance "nothing about us without us" applied to the autism community. This advocacy encourages extensive participation of individuals with autism in the research and development of treatments and assessments to fully understand what causes them actual difficulties versus what symptoms simply make individuals around them uncomfortable. ASAN is in support of more participatory methodologies in research and treatment that encourage exploration of the spaces within and between the neurotypical and neurodivergent worlds. It supports the participation and voices of individuals with autism in the development of treatment and in making decisions about when and whether treatment is necessary. As a case in point, ASAN (2019) advocates for individualized treatment and is opposed to the use of ABA, which is the most common and widely researched treatment for autism. It has argued that ABA was developed by neurotypical individuals and deploys behavioral techniques to help people behave more like neurotypical individuals without appreciating the unique needs and abilities of autistic individuals. For these reasons and others identified above, this book has been reviewed by autistic adults and other therapists, and the therapeutic model featured in Part Two was developed in consultation with folks with autism and in some cases their parents.

AUTISM TRAITS OFTEN TARGETED IN THERAPY

One trait of autism that is often targeted in therapy is that of difficulties with social cognition (APA 2013). These may include difficulties in attributing the emotions of others to events, and instead of attributing relational meanings to social stimuli attention tends to be focused on the periphery (such as noticing the sound of someone's pen clicking rather than what the person is saying). As such, autistic individuals may have difficulty understanding social norms (Bauminger 2002). These difficulties in identifying emotions, when accompanied by RRBs and an interest in peripheral elements, may produce a lack of social motivation (Vismara & Lyons 2007). However, autistic researcher Milton (2012) attributes the social communication difficulties to a "double empathy problem," noting that neurotypical communication partners fail to adapt to those with autism just as those with autism fail to adapt to a neurotypical communication partner. This bolsters the argument that the communication burden/

requirement to change should not solely be placed on autistic people's shoulders.

These social cognition symptoms have been treated through social skills training for individuals with autism. My first job out of art therapy graduate school was running such a program. Proponents of these programs argue that they can assist autistic folks in meeting their goals and provide them (and sometimes neurotypical individuals) with strategies for social communication (Crooke & Winner 2021). However, others criticize these models as unethical attempts to "[train] the autism out of an autistic person" (Roberts 2021, para. 2), and note concerns that this type of treatment can lead to social masking and anxiety. Cassidy and colleagues (2020) found a statistically significant relationship between social masking in college students with autism and suicidal thoughts and behaviors. This again supports the argument that social skills training is harmful to many autistic people and supports Roberts (2021) and the Therapist Neurodiversity Collective's argument that therapists' focus must be shifted to a strengths-based paradigm based in "inclusion, acceptance, empathy, and respect" (para. 18), and one that educates all neurotypes about a wide variety of communication styles rather than a default neurotypical communication. It is of note that Roberts (2021) is an autistic speech language pathologist and the founder of the Therapist Neurodiversity Collective.

Another primary trait of autism spectrum disorder (APA 2013), RRBs, includes various behaviors such as special interests, repetitive motor behavior/stimming, sensory symptoms such as under- or over-stimulation, and difficulty with transitions and/or breaking routine. For example, a child may line up toys in a certain order repeatedly, become excited about this activity and begin flapping their hands, and then become anxious or upset when the family pet knocks over the toys or they are asked to put them away. At this point they may become inconsolable or physically aggressive. These behaviors may frustrate both the individuals with autism and their caregivers; the latter frequently think the former are being stubborn when they are, in fact, having difficulty processing change.

These RRBs are traditionally targeted for change in therapy. Autistic therapy participants are at times punished or taught to do alternative behaviors, as RRBs such as hand flapping are seen as undesirable to others without autism (Raulston & Machalicek 2017). However, if these behaviors are not causing difficulties for the participant with autism, there is no reason to make these the focus of therapy; in fact, it can be more detrimental to autistic participants to discourage these behaviors as they serve a purpose often related to sensory regulation for said participants (Kapp *et al.* 2019).

Special interests, a subtype of RRBs, are defined as high-intensity fixations displayed in individuals with autism (Boyd *et al.* 2007), such as re-watching or memorizing a favorite anime and quoting it over and over. Until recently, therapists attempted to eliminate these RRBs through behavior extinction methods that provided reinforcement for not completing the behaviors and punishment for completing them (Raulston & Machalicek 2017). Treatment of RRBs now varies dependent on type; for instance, those who are self-injurious (for example, repeatedly hitting oneself) are still targeted for modification or elimination, whereas the typical intensity of the perseverative interest subtype, and relative lack of danger to self or others, has led clinicians and researchers to attempt to leverage them as a part of their treatment of social cognitive symptoms (Boyd *et al.* 2007; Raulston & Machalicek 2017; Vismara & Lyons 2007). Bearing in mind the criticisms of social skills training above, it is still relevant to note that Vismara and Lyons (2007) and Boyd *et al.* (2007) found that integrating special interests into social interaction and social skills instruction led to increased social motivation, initiations, and interactions in samples of preschool and early school-age children with autism.

Sensory symptoms are present in autism but historically have been treated as secondary (Boyd *et al.* 2009). Autistic individuals often have sensory hyperreactivity or exaggerated responses to sensations—for example a person who cannot stand the feeling of wet cloth against the skin and therefore immediately removes clothing when it becomes wet. They also frequently experience sensory hyporeactivity, which is the opposite phenomenon. Some individuals with autism are unable to sense extremely hot water temperatures and become burned as a result. Additionally, individuals with autism often display sensory-seeking or sensory-avoiding behaviors, which are often responses to sensory under- or over-stimulation in that they seek out sensory experiences that either fulfill a deficit or remove an unpleasant sensory stimulus.

Researchers have linked sensory hyper- and hyporeactivity and sensory-seeking behavior to special interests and other RRBs in some autistic individuals (Liss *et al.* 2006). In earlier editions of the DSM, sensory symptoms were not included as part of the diagnostic criteria, despite frequent reports by both professionals and parents of sensory hyper- and hyporeactivity and sensory-seeking behavior in individuals with autism (Liss *et al.* 2006). Liss *et al.* (2006) hypothesized that sensory hyperarousal may indeed be responsible for special interests and difficulty in shifting attention between tasks. They surveyed and interviewed approximately 200 parents of autistic individuals to evaluate, based on their reports, whether special interests and behavior resulted from sensory hyperreactivity. They found correlations that supported their hypothesis, which connected sensory hyperarousal to special interests and behavior and selective attention (for example, becoming preoccupied with small details, such as a minute paint stain on a table, to the exclusion of anything else in the room); however, they did not investigate the causation of this connection. Liss *et al.* (2006) also found a correlation between hypoarousal and special interests and behavior and the occurrence of selective attention. It is important to note, however, that they interviewed parents and not the autistic individuals themselves, so the results may be less valid than as presented. Despite this, the study findings suggest that special interests and behaviors may be a gateway to engagement for autistic individuals, particularly when they are experiencing sensory processing difficulties. This also can be interpreted as an argument for not attempting to alter

RRBs unless they are causing physical harm to the individual or others, as these RRBs, more specifically special interests in this example, serve as a coping skill.

Co-occurring anxiety disorders are common in individuals with autism (Kreslins, Robertson, & Melville 2015), and Sze and Wood (2007) noted that this is particularly true of individuals with high-functioning autism. Autistic children have higher rates of anxiety diagnosis than peers without autism. This demographic also has higher rates of obsessive-compulsive disorder (OCD), social anxiety, and specific phobias, although sometimes symptoms are difficult to distinguish because of the similarity with autism symptoms, such as RRB and obsessive thoughts. Individuals with autism and co-occurring anxiety often have difficulty with social relationships that can affect multiple areas of their lives. Therefore, treatment of the underlying anxiety might help to address social skills challenges and other relational difficulties (Sze & Wood 2007). Because RRBs may be a sign of anxiety (Sze & Wood 2007), a professional may encourage engagement of these behaviors to further understand the therapy participant's anxiety, possibly identifying the anxiety's etiology or working toward more adaptive coping skills if the RRB is disruptive or harmful. Based on my clinical experience and on consideration of the feedback of individuals with autism, I would argue that anxiety is often the appropriate focus of treatment. Autism merely gives therapists input as to what ways of working will be most appropriate and effective with autistic participants who also have anxiety or other co-occurring mental health diagnoses.

POSITIVE AUTISM SELF-IDENTITY

Cooper, Smith, and Russell (2017) completed social psychological research into the concept of positive autism self-identity, finding that "Autism identification was positively associated with personal self-esteem through its association with collective self-esteem, and in turn, was negatively associated with depression and anxiety" (2017, p.851). This positive autism identity included a positive personal identity encompassing the autism diagnosis as well as an identity as a member of a community of other autistic people with positive autism identities. Based on their research, Cooper *et al.* suggest that therapists work from a strengths-based positive autism frame to help promote increased self-esteem.

SO NOW WHAT?

Therapists working with autistic folks must be aware of the DSM-defined characteristics of autism and the perspectives of autistic people themselves. Individuals with autism should be actively engaged in their treatment planning whenever possible, just as clinicians would be with most other participants. Therapists must also be familiar with the work of autism self-advocates. What is featured here is a very small portion of the literature written by and in consultation with autistic people. For more information, please check out the Therapist Neurodiversity Collective and Autism Self Advocacy Network (see Chapter 13).

The following chapter provides an overview of the history of autism in psychology, relevant psychological theories, and common therapies for folks with autism, and explores further the problematic nature of some of these approaches.

CHAPTER 3

Autism and Therapy

As noted by the concerns of ASAN (2017, 2019) and the Therapist Neurodiversity Collective (Roberts 2021), psychological theories and therapies with respect to working with autistic people have historically failed to take into account input from autistic individuals. These therapies have often attempted to make participants with autism behave more like those without autism. This chapter provides a brief history of influential psychological theories and therapies for autistic participants.

PSYCHOANALYSIS, ATTACHMENT, AND INTERSUBJECTIVITY

Psychoanalysis

An interest in human development, particularly child development, has been part of Western psychology for at least the last 150 years. In Freud's theory of psychoanalysis and early psychological theory, professionals treated the infant as "a closed system, self-contained and ruled by inner impulses" (Schermer 2000, p.201). Freud saw humans as ruled by their unconscious minds. He asserted that unconscious impulses, memories, and desires govern all human action (Kenney 2014). According to drive theory, these unconscious feelings guide human behavior. The primary human drives, in Freud's estimation, are sex, aggression, and survival. Freud saw the helplessness of infancy as a traumatic experience that was unavoidable and something that parents could not prevent; as such, he believed his views of the human experience to be universal (Kenney 2014). The most social aspect of Freud's theory was the concept of transference, in which he theorized that in order to work through one's intrapsychic issues, especially those stemming from infancy, a patient will transfer unconscious feelings from early experiences with parents and caregivers to the therapist who, in turn, reveals and interprets them. Transference is still very much an unconscious process (Kenney 2014).

Freud described early infancy as a "normal autistic phase" of development, which Mahler (as cited in Mahler, Pine, & Bergman 1975) expanded on. She explained that a newborn's primary contact with the outside world is to meet their physiological needs, such as feeding; otherwise, the newborn remains mostly internally focused, sleeping much of the time. Mahler also posited that children are in "a stage of absolute primary narcissism, marked by a lack of awareness of a mothering agent" (Mahler *et al.* 1975, p.42). Narcissism, in this sense, has to do with self-absorption in the absence of a fully formed construct of the other. The self and other are merged and as yet undifferentiated. While not fully recognizing the caregiver as separate from the self, the infant also senses an inability to fulfill their physiological needs. This nonsocial "autistic" phase eventually gives way to a "normal symbiotic phase" (Mahler *et al.* 1975, p.43) whereby the infant becomes emotionally attached to the caregiver, and begins to recognize the self as existing in a mutually reinforcing system with the caregiver. Mahler *et al.* (1975) asserted that these early phases were the first steps in a process of separation and individuation of the self from the caregiving object on which the infant is completely dependent. The description of these behaviors in early infancy is not unlike the described behavior of individuals with Level 3 autism. Interestingly, Bergman (2000) explained that Mahler eventually rejected Freud's theory of a "normal autistic phase," deciding instead that symbiotic behavior, in which parent and child are intimately co-relational, occurs much earlier in development.

Further developing the ideas of Freud and other psychodynamic theorists, Bettelheim (1967), a mid-20th-century psychoanalyst, theorized that autism arose from "refrigerator mothers" who failed to provide adequate care and loving to their children. He advocated for the removal of autistic children from their birth homes to place them away from "inadequate" parenting. Bettelheim was later discredited as a psychoanalyst as his educational background was in art history and not psychoanalysis (Pollak 1997). Mahler and Furer (1968), however, also espoused similar concepts regarding the origin of autism.

Attachment and intersubjectivity theories

Further development of attachment theory, an offshoot of psychoanalysis, has helped us to better understand the role of attachment in autism. *Attachment* refers to "an affectional tie that one person (or animal) forms to another specific individual. Attachment is thus discriminating and specific" (Salter Ainsworth 1969, p.971) and influences behavior. For example, when children fall and are uninjured, they look around to see if anyone has seen them fall; often when someone has observed the fall they mirror back that person's reaction. If a parent (or other figure to whom the child is attached) appears upset, the child is more likely to cry. If the person is unalarmed, the child is more likely to be unalarmed as well and able to continue engaging in the previous activity.

A central construct in our knowledge of attachment is that behaviors only occur in relationship with others (Salter Ainsworth 1989). Babies are born with instinctual actions, such as crying when hungry, which signal the need for caregiver contact, the result of which helps to establish a reciprocal relationship through mutual cuing. As development proceeds, the infant directs these behaviors less generally and more precisely at specific attachment figures, such as the primary caregiver. As also established in object relations theory, attachment must occur for human survival; however, attachment can take on distinct qualities through either secure or insecure reactions and responses (Salter Ainsworth *et al.* 1978). Securely attached children use their caregivers as a grounding or safe point of reference, which allows them to mitigate anxiety and feel free to explore their environment as well as trust that their caregivers will be present upon their return for emotional refueling. Secure children may become upset if the caregiver leaves their presence, although they generally calm quickly and are content with the idea that the caregiver will, in fact, return. Insecurely attached children, by contrast, feel they cannot count on their caregiver, for whatever reason, to be present and available to return to, and therefore display more emotionally erratic behavior. Healthy attachment forms when children feel safe and have their physical and emotional needs met despite inevitable occasional discomfort or failure (Bowlby 1958).

Intersubjectivity is one of the most recent elaborations from attachment and object relations theories. Intersubjectivity asserts that the self exists in relationship to other selves, which together form an intersubjective field (Benjamin 1988). In its most basic sense, intersubjectivity is emotional reciprocity in human relationships (Gillespie & Cornish 2009); more specifically, intersubjectivity is the often unspoken sharing of feelings between two minds (Benjamin 1988). Stolorow and Atwood (1996), in their development of intersubjectivity theory, also looked to the unconscious but they focused on affective states and the learning of emotions rather than on sexual and survival drives. The reciprocal affective relationship, even on the unconscious level, constitutes a system: "It is not the isolated individual mind...but the larger system created by the mutual interplay between the subjective worlds of patient and analyst, or of child and caregiver" that constitutes the focus of therapy (Stolorow & Atwood 1996, p.182).

The sub-theory of *developmental intersubjectivity* identifies the intersubjective relationship with the primary caregiver from which infants begin to individuate (Benjamin 1998). Benjamin (1998) also theorized that an infant seeks validation from the caregiver and therefore looks to the caregiver to affirm feelings and provide safety and comfort. For instance, an infant may draw a caregiver's attention to a preferred toy by pushing it toward the caregiver or shaking it and looking back at the person. In ideal situations, when either the child cues the caregiver in this way or when the caregiver responds by mirroring these emotions, a reciprocal relationship results in attunement and the sharing of experience and emotions. In this example the caregiver might look at the toy and perhaps even physically interact with it, then mirror back the perceived feeling the infant has regarding the toy. This response creates their joint attention on an object and promotes relationship development as well as overall development of the infant. Not only are both infant and caregiver active participants in such an intersubjective relationship, but also attunement cannot occur without their social interaction (Benjamin 1998). This concept is reminiscent of Winnicott's (1971) transitional space and transitional objects.

Autistic individuals have attachment relationships and intersubjective experiences that are more complicated than these theories might suggest. Children with autism are at higher risk for insecure attachment patterns due to the social and relational symptoms of autism (McKenzie & Dallos 2017). Individuals with autism may also display attachment and behavior patterns that are similar to individuals with reactive attachment disorder (McKenzie & Dallos 2017), although this condition results from abuse and neglect, particularly in the crucial early childhood period. Early on in autism research and diagnostic taxonomy, attachment difficulties in children with autism were similarly attributed to lack of attention and caring interactions, such as hugging and playing, from the mother (Cutler 2004; Kanner 1949; Silberman 2015), but it has since been shown that these patterns result from social communication difficulties that are often inherent in the child from birth (McKenzie & Dallos 2017; Slade 2009), such as a lack of naturally occurring joint attention, decreased eye contact, and other sensory-related characteristics such as disliking touch.

Although these developmental theories are arguably believed to be universal to all children, there are myriad varieties of human behavior, and such theories may be less applicable, as originally conceived, to children with autism. For example, a child who is over-stimulated by a caregiver's loving attention may "shut down" and thereby be perceived by the parent as rejecting the attention. Rejection, in turn, may lead to greater stress in the relationship and exacerbate the attachment difficulties that began with the child's symptomology. Achieving secure attachment with individuals with autism thus requires greater adaptive attention from the caregiver to prevent systemic misinformation or lack of attunement (McKenzie & Dallos 2017; Slade 2009).

Child-centered play therapy

Child-centered play therapy (CCPT) is a form of nondirective play therapy that addresses some of the challenges described above for autistic children, with implications for how therapy may need to be adapted. Specifically, CCPT permits the child to lead the session, based on the notion that with a child-centered, nurturing environment, children will naturally address their emotional and behavioral needs through metaphor (Guerney 2001). This nurturing environment facilitates healthy attachment and promotes the development of self-concept as well as emotional and behavioral regulation (Salter, Beamish, & Davies 2016).

The holding space (Winnicott 1971) that the therapist provides in CCPT facilitates the child's completion of developmental stages at the child's pace; these stages may not have been previously completed due to the child's symptomology (Salter *et al.* 2016). CCPT emphasizes attachment through promotion of joint attention as the child and therapist explore the child's interests together. CCPT also encourages social learning through therapist imitation and modeling related to the child's initiations. This supportive play environment encourages development of verbal skills and social development (Salter *et al.* 2016).

Salter *et al.* (2016) conducted a single-case design research study with three participants with autism in Australia. They assessed social and emotional progress (as well as parental perceptions of progress).

All three participants showed measurable, albeit nonlinear, progress, which suggests that CCPT may be effective for autistic participants. Overley and colleagues (2018) interviewed 10 registered play therapists trained in CCPT, who noted that the neutral environment of the CCPT playroom provided a welcoming atmosphere, and the sameness and consistency of the environment provided autistic children with a sense of comfort as well as a sense of control. These outcomes in turn facilitated the children's empowerment to make their own decisions.

The play therapists interviewed by Overley *et al.* (2018) claimed that the CCPT process facilitated relationship development through nurturing a nondirective, child-focused atmosphere, which parents reported had helped their children generalize relationship skills in their interactions with peers. Other important factors in the CCPT process of relationship development included therapist attunement with the child through following the child's lead, a lack of adult redirection of play, unconditional acceptance of the child, and a willingness to learn from the child (for example, what the child's interests are, what makes the child comfortable, etc.) as important relationship builders/guides to therapeutic goals. The therapist's willingness to provide caregiver support, psychoeducation, and training also constitutes an important part of CCPT with autistic children, and extends the effects of CCPT beyond the therapeutic relationship (Guerney 2001; Overley *et al.* 2018).

Because CCPT is child-directed, there are no specific procedures that therapists follow other than providing unconditional acceptance and a willingness to learn from the child (Overley *et al.* 2018), as well as social modeling through a nurturing environment (Salter *et al.* 2016). These characteristics make it difficult to validate or test the research, not only because of small sample sizes, but also because of the open-ended procedures structure. However, these studies do suggest that following the client's lead may be a productive way to work with autistic individuals, which supports the advocacy goals of ASAN (2015; Ne'eman 2012).

Joint attention

Another therapeutic concept worth reviewing here is joint attention. Kasari, Freeman, and Paparella (2006) conducted a pretest/posttest study in which young autistic children were engaged in either joint attention skills or imaginative play that included observation and imitation. The researchers compared the two intervention groups to a control group and found that children in the intervention groups gained these skills by a statistically significant margin. Other researchers have investigated whether introducing children's special interests into social situations with peers could increase their use of joint attention skills in engagement with peers (Boyd *et al.* 2007; Koegel *et al.* 2012; Vismara & Lyons 2007). In these studies participants' interests were largely derived from popular culture, including areas such as movie trivia, comic books and gaming, and card games. Researchers observed increased social engagement with neurotypical peers and decreased social isolation. These studies lend support to my supposition that engaging special interests can build the therapeutic relationship and also help participants with autism to participate and communicate in the neurotypical world within which they live.

COGNITIVE BEHAVIORAL THERAPY

Cognitive therapy laid the foundation for the creation of cognitive behavioral therapy (CBT), a well-documented, short-term treatment that targets problematic thoughts to improve or change behavior (Beck 2011). Like psychodynamic forms of therapy, cognitive therapy and CBT maintain focus on the individual (Beck 2011), although at times this involves challenging negative thoughts about social interactions. However, unlike psychodynamic treatments before them, cognitive therapy and CBT have been found to relieve symptoms relatively quickly, in weeks, rather than years. This difference is one of the reasons such treatment has become quite popular in mental health care agencies. Moreover, extensive and rigorous research has helped to demonstrate the success of CBT in short-term therapy settings as compared to other treatment and placebos (David, Cristea, & Hoffman 2018). David *et al.* (2018) argued that CBT became the gold standard in therapy because most other forms of therapy were not researched as thoroughly, with equally accepted experimental methods of measuring effectiveness and efficacy.

Therapists often implement CBT as the preferred method of treatment for typically developing children with anxiety disorders (Sze & Wood 2007). CBT aims at changing thinking patterns and behaviors through how one recognizes the problematic results of said patterns and behaviors (Lang *et al.* 2010). For instance, if a client is afraid of entering a social situation, a therapist might ask what thoughts are behind that fear. After identifying the thoughts, the therapist would ask the client to challenge those thoughts and think of alternative outcomes for the anxiety-provoking situation.

CBT was not developed as a therapy specifically for autistic people; rather, it exists as a treatment for accompanying anxiety and other mental health issues (Creed 2015). Autistic individuals often have difficulty with abstract thought and impaired social insight (Attwood 2004), and may therefore have more difficulty applying CBT processes, so therapists adjust these to increase success. One adolescent I worked with knew that people liked jokes, so he would tell a joke he found really funny. People did not laugh, but he did not appear to notice and continued to tell the joke repeatedly to the same people. As a result of this, people began to avoid him socially. He did not understand what had gone wrong because he had followed the "rule" that people like jokes. His difficulty understanding the social impact of his behavior was likely due to a lack of understanding of the social cues of his peers' body language or social language, as well as a lack of insight into his own behavior. However, in the context of the criticisms of social skills training in the previous chapter, it is also important to point out that his peers also did not recognize or attempt to understand his cues either, or if they did, they responded to it with body language rather than vocally. They could have taken the content of the joke as a sign of a good topic for conversation with this young man.

Researchers have completed systematic reviews of the literature to understand the usefulness of CBT for anxiety with autistic people (Kreslins *et al.* 2015; Lang *et al.* 2010). Kreslins *et al.* (2015) reviewed 30 studies with approximately 500 participants and noted from the self-reports included in these studies that caregivers and clinicians found the treatment to be successful; the participants themselves, however, did not always agree with this assessment. This discrepancy might be due to the language and cognitive abilities of the participants, or it may indicate that the criteria for what was considered to be successful treatment differed between the caregivers and the participants. Regardless of the positivity of the caregivers, there may be a need to adapt how CBT is delivered to individuals with autism. The review by Kreslins *et al.* (2015) highlighted input from individuals with autism as to their feelings about a treatment method. However, they also recommended the use of CBT despite the negative response from individuals with autism. This discrepancy suggests a need for further consultation with individuals with autism regarding their treatment, especially in conjunction with recommendations from neurodiversity advocates.

Systematic reviews note that the existing literature frequently only addresses working with individuals with Level 1 or Level 2 autism (previously called high-functioning autism or Asperger syndrome) and not individuals with greater apparent difficulties in functioning, such as Level 3 autism (Kreslins *et al.* 2015; Lang *et al.* 2010). Lang *et al.* (2010), who examined nine studies, theorized that this research and practice bias might relate to verbal and cognitive differences across the spectrum: individuals with Level 1 autism are generally more verbally expressive and produce a greater expectation among practitioners that they are able to participate in CBT, which tends to be a verbally complex therapy that requires talking through problematic thoughts and countering those thoughts. There is less expectation that individuals who are minimally verbal, as those with

Level 3 autism often are, will be able to understand the CBT process. Both studies report that CBT appeared to be an effective treatment for more verbal study participants, as reported by caregivers (Kreslins *et al.* 2015; Lang *et al.* 2010).

The systematic reviews by Lang *et al.* (2010) and Kreslins *et al.* (2015) both illustrate areas that ASAN (2017; Ne'eman 2012) has criticized regarding therapies for individuals with autism. The development and testing of the effectiveness of these therapies rely heavily on the input of neurotypical caregivers, teachers, and providers of those with autism, and may discount the desires and input of the individuals with autism themselves. The same criticism could apply to what Bauminger (2002) mentioned, as discussed previously. Strevett-Smith's (2010) case study involved a child with autism more actively in developing the course and execution of therapy.

Attwood (2004) suggested adaptations of CBT for individuals with autism to overcome insight, language, and social impairments that might otherwise make CBT difficult or less successful. His suggestion was based on his interactions with and observations of his participants and his sister-in-law, who were diagnosed with autism outside of these observations. It is unclear whether he gathered input from individuals with autism. He recommended making visual examples, such as drawing out how to interact in social situations or other anxiety-provoking situations, or presenting a comic or storyboard showing someone telling a joke only one time and showing a variety of social responses. Other examples include pictures and scrapbooks that make social expectations more tangible, such as a picture of a row of urinals with men standing at every other urinal, as depicted by Baker (2006), to help a client understand bathroom etiquette. Still other examples include writing social stories, a concept developed by Gray (1994), in which a story or comic strip is tailored to specific situations to help individuals anticipate what will be expected of them socially.

Integrating special interests into these methods can help increase interest and engagement on the part of participants with autism. Sze and Wood (2007) illustrated this point with a case example of a preadolescent girl with autism. She enjoyed drawing and was preoccupied with fears of kidnapping and war (possibly related to her interest in the *Star Wars* movie series), so the therapists asked her to draw what war looked like to her and then utilized another interest, Indiana Jones, to save the day. Her parents also trained in how to assist their daughter in applying her coping skills. The researchers noted that after treatment she no longer met the criteria for the three anxiety disorders. Unlike the previously mentioned examples, Sze and Wood (2007) outlined how they specifically worked with the girl's interests to facilitate her ability to lessen her anxiety, more in line with what ASAN (2015; Ne'eman 2012) has suggested as a better practice in therapy.

APPLIED BEHAVIOR ANALYSIS

Applied behavior analysis (ABA) is a form of behavior therapy that also utilizes some cognitive theory principles, specifically those related to typical child development. ABA was developed in the mid-20th century and is based on models of operant conditioning to teach desired behaviors (academic skill, impulse control, etc.) and to decrease undesired behaviors (Kearney 2015). ABA has garnered the support of a wide variety of state and federal agencies in the US as a well-researched and effective treatment for autism symptoms (Hagopian, Hardesty, & Gregory 2015). Despite this praise, ABA is controversial, largely due to the early use of electroshock therapy and other physical punishments to decrease unwanted behavior (Silberman 2015), but also related to reports from individuals with autism that they have been damaged by this therapy. ASAN (2015) wrote a letter to the US Department of Education's Special Education Department to encourage schools and associated agencies to not see ABA as a one-size-fits-all treatment because of documented ethical concerns, and also what ASAN viewed as use of ABA to the exclusion of other treatments that might be more appropriate, such as speech and language therapy.

ABA generally uses rewards and punishments to increase or decrease specific identified behaviors, which are the basic tenets of operant conditioning (Lovaas Institute 2018). The most commonly followed and researched approach, the Lovaas Model, is applied in early childhood, generally between the ages of two and eight, often for between 20 and 40 hours per week. For young children, the goals of ABA include physical and verbal imitation, language development, and play development. For older children, more focus is placed on self-care and socialization. This is often done through discrete trial training, which includes the "teacher" demonstrating or providing an instruction for a behavior and the child imitating or completing the behavior and repeating this process until the child no longer needs to rely on all of the physical, verbal, and visual prompts (Lovaas Institute 2018). The child is rewarded at varying intervals for completing the behavior, and encouraged to generalize the behavior to multiple settings through varied practice. Lay therapists (individuals with a Bachelor's degree or college students) who are trained and supervised by a Master's level clinician or consultant often supply this facilitation. The Lovaas Model also involves use of incidental teaching, which encompasses practicing skills away from the typical ABA setting and may integrate peer play (Lovaas Institute 2018). Forty years of research support the Lovaas Model (and other models of ABA). Lovaas (1987) found that 90 percent of children who participated in his model of ABA showed improvement in their skills and behavior, with nearly 50 percent displaying "normal" behavior and IQ after participation.

The Lovaas Model has had an outsized influence on autism treatment. To offer my own experience as an example, as a lay practitioner I recall being told that ABA could make children with autism indistinguishable from their neurotypical peers, and that the goal was to shape them to have typical behavior and academic skills. Although there are clearly some advantages to this goal, particularly for academic development and, to a lesser degree, social functioning, the prevailing opinion of professionals in the 1960s through the early

2000s emphasized a neurotypical lens on autism. Desirable social behavior is entirely contingent on what neurotypical individuals define it as, and not on what neurodivergent individuals feel or desire. The latter's ability to communicate this desire is not always evident, however, given that ABA treatment begins in early childhood, before a child has acquired a repertoire of communication skills.

ABA is a thoroughly researched and successful therapy, but ASAN's (2015) concern over ABA being treated as a one-size-fits-all treatment is more than valid, based on the literature and clinical observations of therapists in various fields in addition to many testimonials from autistic folks. In the intervening years between my work as a lay therapist with ABA and my subsequent training as a certified, Master's level clinical consultant in ABA, I also completed two Master's degrees in the professions of art therapy and mental health counseling and worked in a recreation therapy program. My training and direct observations gave me a healthy dose of skepticism for exclusive use of ABA. This led me to develop a more integrated approach as an ABA consultant, working with art therapy interns who learned both ABA and non-ABA methods that offered a more flexible approach, decreasing the rigidity of the approach and being sensitive to the input of and desires of the autistic participants. This involved focusing mostly on academic goals and providing plenty of time for child-directed art and play.

There is some research support for adapting ABA in a way that is tailored to individual needs. Camargo *et al.* (2016) conducted a meta-analysis of behaviorally oriented social skills development programs in inclusive settings (involving individuals with and without autism), many of which utilize ABA methods. The researchers examined 19 studies that measured outcomes from common components of ABA including reinforcement, modeling, prompting, and direct instruction to teach social skills. They found that behavioral methods were effective in teaching social skills, and planned reinforcement worked better than natural reinforcement. Both natural and planned modeling and natural and planned prompting were equally effective.

They also found that it did not matter whether researchers, teachers, peers, or others provided the instruction; all were equally effective. Problematically, however, success was defined by individuals without autism, and there is some evidence that social skills training programs may promote suicidal feelings through encouraging social masking (Cassidy *et al.* 2020; Roberts 2021).

SO WHAT CAN THERAPISTS DO TO REMEDIATE OR AVOID HARM IN THE THERAPEUTIC RELATIONSHIP?

Historically theories and therapies directed at autistic folks have been framed from a neurotypical lens. Therapy goals have generally been set to help autistic participants mask their autism, which can lead to suicidal thoughts and actions. It is important for contemporary clinicians to understand the history of theory and treatment as well as to consider the testimonials of therapy participants with autism. Although social skills training and ABA have proven successful in therapy researcher and associated literature, that research is most often from a non-autistic perspective. If therapists are to truly work from a "do no harm" approach, they must consider the impact of the therapy they are applying, and whether the intent and goals of the therapy are truly for the benefit of autistic participants. Therapists must, where possible, engage autistic participants in developmentally appropriate discussions of therapy, and encourage these folks to set their own goals rather than consulting a parent or other professionals involved with the case. Additionally, therapists can help non-autistic family members and friends also change and adapt their behavior, rather than putting the burden fully on those with autism.

CHAPTER 4

Art Therapy and Autism

Art therapy practice is diverse, with approaches rooted in most psychological/counseling theories as well as neuroscience and anthropology as well as art therapy-specific theories. Much of the literature on art therapy and autism describes practices aimed at treating symptoms such as social and behavioral concerns, but attachment and sensory integration are also a common focus. This chapter provides a brief synopsis of these approaches with a particular focus on attachment, as much of special interest communication theory (SICT) is concerned with relationship development. Finally, the chapter includes a description of art therapy literature that emphasizes or provides examples of participant autonomy in the process.

The most commonly mentioned outcomes with autistic individuals in the art therapy literature, at the time of this publication, are improvements in communication (Betts, Harmer, & Schumelevich 2014; Isserow 2008; Martin 2008, 2009; Regev & Snir 2013), improved emotional expression (Betts *et al.* 2014; Durrani 2014; Elkis-Abuhoff 2008; Martin 2008, 2009; Regev & Snir 2013), improved self-image (Betts *et al.* 2014; Elkis-Abuhoff 2008, 2009; Regev & Snir 2013), greater flexibility of thought and behavior (Betts *et al.* 2014; Regev & Snir 2013; Schweizer 1997), greater behavioral control (Betts *et al.* 2014; Schweizer, Knorth, & Spreen, 2014), and physical development (such as hand–eye coordination; see Betts *et al.* 2014). Many commonly noted goals for autistic folks in art therapy are rooted in addressing the identified symptoms of autism, which may be appropriate if these symptoms cause distress in the autistic participant; working from the stated goals of the autistic participant is ideal, just as it is in working with any other population.

Studies taking into account the sum of art therapists' experiences working with individuals with autism also highlight these areas of focus (Schweizer *et al.* 2014; Schweizer, Spreen, & Knorth 2017; Schweizer *et al.* 2020; Van Lith, Stallings, & Harris 2017). Koo and Thomas (2019) conducted and evaluated the effects of art therapy with a focus on autism symptoms with nine children in India using the Childhood Autism Rating Scale (CARS; see Schopler, Reichler, & Renner 1988). They describe the CARS as follows:

> There are 15 criteria including relating to people, imitation, emotional response, body, object use, adaptation to change, visual response, listening response, taste–smell–touch response and use, fear and nervousness, verbal communication, nonverbal communication, activity level, level and consistency of intellectual response, and general impressions. (Koo & Thomas 2019, p.210)

Koo and Thomas (2019) explain that they customized the art therapy sessions for each child and encouraged free choice of art supplies, with the facilitator providing some education about art elements and encouraging motor skills and imagination practice. They found a statistically significant improvement in autism symptoms after participation in art therapy.

As the purpose of this book is to explore how special interests build relationships with autistic participants, this chapter focuses more specifically on art therapy and attachment/relationship building in the therapeutic relationship, and on literature that highlights following the lead of participants with autism.

ATTACHMENT AND THE THERAPEUTIC RELATIONSHIP WITH AUTISTIC PARTICIPANTS AND THEIR ART

Springham and Huet (2018) noted the importance of attachment in therapeutic relationships and proposed the ostensive communication theory of art therapy to assist in explaining this relationship in art therapy. They posit that art serves as ostensive communication, as without social context, art is merely an object. Therefore, focus on the art in art therapy offers "powerful mirroring opportunities" that promote an attachment relationship between artist and art therapist by "decreas[ing] the risk of the relational encounter becoming too intense" (Springham & Huet 2018, p.9). The art therapist must attune to the client and the client's artwork to help successfully forge a trusting relationship, and Springham and Huet (2018) provide an example of this from Evans and Dubowski's (2001) accounts of art therapy with children with autism.

Martin (2009) noted that art (and art therapy) helps build relationships by providing a point of joint attention for the therapist and the child with autism, also noting the art process is often intrinsically rewarding to the child. Durrani (2014, 2019, 2021) and Martin (2009) observed that art therapy is helpful in addressing sensory difficulties (such as tactile defensiveness or regression related to sensations). Durrani (2014, 2019, 2021) and Dolphin, Byers, Goldsmith, and Jones (2014) also recognized the importance of the art process in forming attachments in the art therapeutic relationship.

Durrani (2019, p.136) further states:

> Art therapy can facilitate attachment between child and art therapist because it involves multisensory experiences employed within a relational context. An art therapist can use the subjective qualities of art materials to induce sensory regulation in a child with autism and open the path for forming a healthy relationship both through the process of attunement and sensory-based relational art making. The relational aim of the art therapy session, is for the therapist

to become the secure base for the child to explore art making at a comfortable level, which requires a highly attuned, empathic understanding of the child's needs.

Sensory-based art therapy

Durrani (2021) further describes her theory and procedure of the sensory-based relational art therapy approach (S-BRATA), arguing a greater need for a focus on emotional wellbeing for autistic individuals, and notes that this is often absent from the more common behavioral approaches for working with autistic individuals. Durrani (2021) emphasizes the importance of recognizing the pervasiveness of sensory integration dysfunction despite its frequent absence from diagnostic criteria for autism. She describes how sensory integration difficulties can interfere with attachment in early childhood, and argues the need for encouraging secure attachment in children with autism due to the documented psychoemotional benefits of secure attachment. Art therapy is well suited to address both sensory integration and attachment simultaneously through use of sensory art to assist with self-regulation, which then opens the autistic participant to secure attachment. Durrani (2021) notes seven themes or types of therapist participant interaction of the S-BRATA that help with sensory regulation and attachment and therefore promote emotional wellbeing:

1. Safety built through co-regulation, with the art therapist's self-regulation providing a means of regulation for the child.
2. Accommodating the sensory profile of the child.
3. "Art materials as entry point for engagement" (Durrani 2021, p.80)—use of nontraditional media.
4. Use of mirroring and attunement in joint art making to form attachment.

5. Utilizing a flexible approach—openness to non-visual media/non-traditional methods and surfaces.

6. Maintaining a level of structure and boundaries.

7. Not making art product the focus/focal point—it's okay to not have a tangible product.

These seven themes provide a loose framework for addressing sensory integration and attachment to build relationships with autistic children. Durrani (2021) is sensory- and process-focused, which is rather contrary to the often insight-oriented approaches in art therapy.

Triadic relationship

Relatedly, Edwards (2014) noted that it is commonly accepted in art therapy that success in participation is due to the triangular relationship between art therapist, client artist, and artwork. Dolphin and colleagues (2014) asserted that the triangular relationship is paramount in the therapeutic relationship with individuals with autism in art therapy, with a particular focus on the transference/countertransference dynamic and the client as lead in the therapy session. They emphasize the role of art in providing a point of joint reflection and lowering the intensity of the therapeutic interaction to a manageable level for autistic individuals. Durrani (2014) described a case study detailing art therapy with a 12-year-old autistic boy named Tom. Durrani noted that Tom had a difficult attachment history due to family conflict and the symptoms of autism itself, in particular sensory stimulation avoidance. She mirrored Tom's interactions with art materials, in an effort to encourage attunement in the relationship. Durrani observed that Tom gradually became less tactile-resistant as the therapeutic relationship strengthened. She also noted improved self-regulation over the course of the sessions. Martin (2008) observed similar relationship building through a portrait-drawing process. Arguably, she also encouraged attunement through the steps of mutual portrait drawing; she observed improved eye contact and social investment on the part of her study participants. Elkis-Abuhoff (2008, 2009) also described increased interpersonal relationships over the course of the art therapeutic process with two adolescents with Asperger syndrome.

Durrani (2014) and Isserow (2008, 2013) suggested that if the art therapist is willing to mirror what the child is doing (rather than the reverse) through sensory-based art, attachment relationships can be facilitated. Isserow (2013) posited that a therapist's mirroring of a child's art process promoted attunement, attachment, and self-regulation in children with autism. Isserow (2008, 2013) also suggested that the triadic relationship of art, client, and therapist serves to build joint attention as well as provide an opening to the development of the therapeutic alliance. The case of a participant he called Mary had a diagnosis of autism, was nonverbal, and appeared unable to relate one-on-one with the therapist, which suggested difficulties in early development of object relations. However, Isserow (2008) reported some success in relating through joint art production:

> Mary's capacity to relate triadically seemed to be a considerable developmental achievement away. Working with her highlighted the enormity and importance of the need to establish a shared experience with the other, in order for a therapeutic relationship to develop. (2008, p.39)

The creation of a joint object by the art therapist and client thus provided a focus for joint attention and helped to build attunement and thereby a foundation for a therapeutic relationship. Attention to a client's special interests, likewise, offers an opportunity to model joint attention and encourage relationship development.

Interactive square

Bragge and Fenner (2009) developed a model of an intersubjective approach to art therapy called the "interactive square," which takes the triadic relationship a step further by including both the art therapist's and the client's artworks in the therapeutic interface or, alternatively, in the creation of joint artwork between the art therapist and client. Moon (1999) also observed that responsive art making facilitated building relationships with adolescent participants. This process includes the art therapist creating art in response to the art of the client and the client themself. Arguably this is true with all participants who respond to art therapy, the reflected art being equated with verbal minimal encouragers in counseling. This process encourages a mutual relationship and empathy. Bragge and Fenner (2009) hypothesized that clinician art making may assist in developing mutual relationships with autistic people. From their review of videotaped sessions of participants' responses while the therapist engaged in responsive art making, they remarked, "Subjective, artistic responses were recognized as particularly appropriate for engaging empathically with the children" (Bragge & Fenner 2009, p.17). They noted the importance of the art therapy being a "mutual, co-creative and intersubjective" process rather than one of analysis and instruction (Bragge & Fenner 2009, p.17). They emphasized that the co-creative process facilitated use of the clinician's subjective experience of sessions to relate to participants and meet their needs. A visual dialogue between therapist, client, client art, and therapist art was created through real-time responsive art making by the therapist. In the development of this approach they acknowledged inspiration in the interactive nature of other creative arts therapies such as drama and dance therapy.

Bragge and Fenner (2009) illustrated their model with two case vignettes. The first, of a highly verbal seven-year-old with autism, illustrated interaction types 1, 2, 3, and 4. First, they observed and expanded on the client's imagery to engage him in expanding his artistic repertoire, much like my own client experiences with popular culture interests. Next, for interaction type 3, the therapist created art and, for interaction type 4, the client and therapist compared their art and subsequently added individual and joint art making or joint attention on the art. Following and concurrent with this process the researchers observed increased verbal sharing from the client. Although he did mention being intimidated by the art therapist researcher's quality of artwork, he continued to accept her encouragement and engage in the sessions.

The second case example, of a nonverbal 12-year-old with autism, began with descriptions of self-stimulatory behavior, spinning, wandering around the room, and exploring the setting and available materials for the first four sessions. Bragge and Fenner (2009) categorized these first sessions as an interaction type 2 (that is, the client and the media interacting without the art therapist). The researcher did not stop the child from this exploration, but rather allowed for individual exploration before mirroring of the child's interaction with the art material in the third session as a process of using special interests to build the therapeutic relationship. Eventually, the child tolerated the researcher sitting next to her while creating art (identified as interaction type 3 because of the therapist's attention to her own artwork). Finally, the client was able to tolerate more direct interaction from the researcher by observing and mirroring the researcher's mark making, although she did later retreat to a corner (interaction type 5). Over time, the client became more playful and interactive.

Bragge and Fenner (2009) concluded that the interactive square model promotes relationship, development/therapeutic alliance, empathy, and communication development in participants with autism, citing the increased communication of both case subjects as evidence for these assertions. They posited that the art of both the therapist and the client provided an external object of focus, which reduced the client's pressure to interact socially. They also asserted that the client-centered nature of the approach was beneficial in helping participants feel connected to the therapist. This mirroring and attuning to client needs supports development of the therapeutic relationship and of joint attention, and provides an insight to the functioning of intersubjectivity within art therapy.

This theory aligns with how I have intuitively facilitated sessions with autistic individuals. Although I will at times divert and direct a session in a more cognitive behavioral direction when necessary, I have generally found it best to follow the client's lead, and use my own art making (either independently as a response to the client or in mirroring the client) to build and encourage client participation. Although the interactive square model could be defined in greater detail, the consideration of how the holding of the therapeutic space, encouragement of exploration, and mirroring of the client all promote attunement is congruent with my experience working with this population.

Relationship building with metaphor

Relationship building with autistic participants also involves attuning to their interests. Henley (1989) described how special interests give art therapists a view into the psyche of individuals with autism, and asserted that if art therapists pay close attention to the repetitive interests of such participants, they will be able to identify the participants' primary concerns. Moon (2007) referred to the art therapist as a *metaphoretician* who "skillfully and spontaneously uses metaphors to uncover and convert truths" and is "inclined to speculative contemplation and action in response to metaphors" (p.12). The greater the ability to stay in the metaphor with the client, the more therapeutic the relationship may become as therapist and autistic participant understand each other and achieve more therapeutic goals (Henley 2018).

In my work this translates into looking for the deeper meaning of the participants' presenting imagery, which may include references from popular culture. In considering this idea I can readily call up the example of a teenage client, whose entire body of artwork was centered on the characters Sonic and Shadow from the "Sonic the Hedgehog" video game franchise. On the surface, his images were mere stereotypic reproductions of these characters. However, after relating with this client over time, I learned that these images, particularly those of Shadow—a character that may be interpreted as Sonic's shadow side—represented how this client chose to interact with the world. He adopted the persona of Shadow as a protection from bullying, and even dressed in the color patterns of Shadow's coat. These images were all about his interaction with the world, not just a game he liked to play.

PROMOTING AGENCY IN ART THERAPY FOR AUTISTIC PARTICIPANTS

Henley (1989, 2018) and Van Lith, Stallings, and Harris (2017) provided case examples encouraging the use of popular culture special interests in engaging autistic participants. The direct engagement of client interests and encouragement of personal agency in the therapy process is necessary in autism positive art therapy. Schweizer *et al.*'s (2020) Delphi study of art therapists also makes mention of the use of special interests as a way to forge relationships and facilitate progress in therapy. They note the importance of being flexible in the art therapy process, and provide an example of encouraging autistic participants to develop special interests/preoccupations into adaptive skills, such as drawing a favorite interest, as a way to reduce stress. Schweizer *et al.* (2020) also note that encouraging artistic exploration of interests cultivates self-expression and emotional regulation through the art therapy process. They provide an example of a child who liked volcanoes, and how, after artistic exploration of volcanoes, the boy connected his own dysregulation to the volcano eruption process (Schweizer *et al.* 2020).

Hartman (2020) used a narrative approach to encourage female adolescents with an autism diagnosis to share their experience of autism and creative narratives of self and disability advocacy and for social inclusion. These artistic narratives were featured in an art show. Hartman noted themes of self and diagnosis acceptance and intersectional identities. Hartman noted that the art therapy group that led to the show provided an outlet for identity exploration and self-expression.

CONCLUSION

Use of art therapy to address symptoms of autism is well documented, as is the ability of the art therapists and art therapy approaches to build therapeutic relationships with children with autism. There is less focus on specific examples of encouraging autonomy in the therapeutic process with autistic participants. This overview of the art therapy literature provides a foundation for the special interest communication theory (SICT). Additionally, the following chapter will provide an overview of historical and contemporary perspectives of digital media and popular media and culture within the practice of art therapy, and specific considerations in the literature for working with autistic children.

CHAPTER 5

Popular Media in Therapy

Digital Methods in Art Therapy and Popular Culture Content and Its Relevance

Historically, when art therapy literature discusses media and materials and autistic participants, these discussions have most often been in the context of sensory media/sensory exploration (Betts *et al.* 2014; Durrani 2014; Isserow 2008, 2013; Kearns 2004; Kuo & Plavnick 2015; Martin 2008, 2009; Regev & Snir 2013) and drawing and traditional art media (Isserow 2008; Martin 2008; Richard, More, & Joy 2015; Van Lith, Stallings & Harris 2017). These discussions have less frequently included electronic and other popular media (Henley 2018; Van Lith, Stallings & Harris 2017). This chapter examines positive and negative perspectives from art therapy and other literature on including electronic and popular media within art therapy sessions.

POPULAR MEDIA AND CULTURE IN ART THERAPY

Twenty years ago, Kramer and colleagues (1997) speculated that the pervasive influence of television at the time affected parent engagement with their children. They asserted that the utilization of "electronic babysitters," such as TV and video games, led to children and adults with dependent personalities and inherent inabilities to self-soothe, form relationships, or fully understand the environments they lived in without instant gratification from electronic media. Kramer *et al.* suggested "that art therapists may be able to help children as well as their young parents to transcend the seduction of technology by introducing them to tangible art materials" (1997, p.108). They theorized that popular electronic media had become substitutes for imagination, relationships, and self-esteem, and therefore they led to a need for instant gratification and an inability to work through problems.

In the intervening years between the observations of Kramer *et al.* (1997) and the present day, digital media have become ubiquitous in the lives of both art therapists and their participants. Looking at a snapshot of technology use in the year 2018, the pervasiveness of technology in US life is clear, but that impact has been different from what Kramer *et al.* predicted. The Pew Research Center conducts frequent surveys to examine the use of technology among US teens. It found that in 2018, 95 percent of a representative sample (ages 13–17) reported access to a smartphone, and 45 percent were constantly online (Anderson & Jiang 2018). These data represent a significant increase from a survey just four years earlier, when only 73 percent had access to a smartphone and 24 percent reported an online presence (Anderson & Jiang 2018). I have observed in my own practice in the last five years, in individuals with and without autism, that problems related to smartphones, computers, tablets, and social media use have become paramount with preteen and teenage participants; many times, the problems relate to access/allowed use and risky behavior, such as talking with strangers or sending nude photos to these people.

Much online participation is on social media platforms, the most popular being YouTube, with 85 percent of survey participants reporting regular use (Anderson & Jiang 2018). YouTube gives people the ability to upload any video content of their choice and to make that content accessible web-wide. Content ranges from TV shows and movies to videos of people playing video games to explicit adult-content videos. At this time, all of my participants use YouTube, and most of them elect to watch videos of others playing video games. They may also use it for other content such as watching sports or learning about preferred toys. Unfortunately, an innocent search on YouTube can turn up developmentally inappropriate content. One child with autism I worked with watched fan fiction videos and became very disturbed by one featuring a My Little Pony dissecting another Pony (which has since been removed from the site). This same child also once told me that he learned to interact with others by reading YouTube comments, which, in turn, led to him cursing and calling people names.

Due to the pervasiveness of digital and social media outlets, art therapists must decide whether to include digital media and popular culture in their practice or exclude them. Orr (2005, 2010, 2012, 2016) has examined and analyzed trends of technology use within the field of art therapy in recent years. In 2005, Orr suggested that due to the increased use of technology among the general population, it was wise to integrate technology into art therapy practice, but at the same time she claimed that art therapists were adopting technology (such as computers, tablets, and smartphones) at lower rates than the general population. However, by 2011, she observed that art therapists had caught up with the general population in technology adoption and use. Orr (2016) compared the initial hesitancy among art therapists to their slow adoption of photography during the first 30 years of the profession, when they focused more on traditional drawing, painting, and sculpting as art media of choice.

Digital technology in the art therapy space

Kapitan (2007) postulated that art therapists' reluctance with digital media may be due to being caught up in the fine art world sentiment that has devalued digital art in favor of traditional media such as drawing and painting: "Traditional art media are regarded by some as more therapeutic than anything produced on the computer or in non-traditional environments" (p.50). Carlton (2014) made similar observations, reporting that, after reviewing related literature, it appeared that art therapists were slow to adopt new media because of historic resistance to "'synthetic' new media" and the preference for "traditional art forms" (p.42). She also noted that cost and a lack of training prevented some art therapists from adopting digital technology. She observed that digital access and use had grown since the dawn of the TV age, and that newly trained art therapists were likely steeped in it. My experience as an art therapist very much fits these reports: I obtained my Master's degree in 2005 at the age of 25, and had been utilizing computers for 20 years at that point. As a faculty member in an art therapy program, I also observed an increasing number of students with digital art degrees.

Gerity (2001) and her supervisees observed that participants and other children they knew were exhibiting demands to be passively entertained, were restless, and had a preference for electronic activities such as video games and TV, and also complained of boredom when these demands were not met. According to Gerity, this desire for near-constant entertainment leads to feelings of emptiness in both adults and children. She emphasized that the virtual "seductive environment" provides a challenge for art therapists in client engagement as well as for participants in everyday life (Gerity 2001, p.44). These concerns have been validated, as research demonstrates changes in brain function related to exposure to technology, both in early (Vandewater *et al.* 2006) and late (Small *et al.* 2009) life. Therefore, art therapists in practice are challenged to adapt and integrate the positive aspects of technology use and counter the negative influences (Kapitan 2009). Gerity emphasized the need for art therapy and art spaces themselves to provide a transitional space between the popular culture media experience, the immediate environment, and the inner self. She chose to accomplish this by continuing to use traditional media rather than adopting digital media.

Klorer (2009) supported the idea of keeping the art therapy session a technology-free space. She asserted that art therapists must acknowledge and address the detriments technology could have, particularly on children and adolescent participants. She had observed increased attentional and interpersonal difficulties in her participants, which she saw as stemming from frequent use of technology and increased interaction via social media and text messages rather than by speaking in person or by telephone. Orr (2010) noted idiosyncrasies in participants' use of digital media for social interaction, observing that digital media can simultaneously decrease and increase social isolation.

Klorer (2009) strove to assist participants in striking a balance between technological interaction and one-on-one, in-person interaction. She saw danger in the use of technology in the session where "art becomes another imitative shorthand that echoes the world the child lives in" (Klorer 2009, p.82), rather than providing an enriching and engaging experience for the child or adolescent client. Klorer, like Gerity (2001), utilized the art therapy session as a transitional space. On the other hand, Thong (2007) concluded, as had Parker-Bell (1999), that digital art making was valid for therapeutic use and can promote the therapeutic relationship, particularly with individuals who have experienced tactile aversions and with digital natives (those who have used technology from a young age; see Prensky 2001). Thong observed in her professional experience that children were just as successful in their therapeutic goals when using digital media as when using traditional media.

Orr (2010) asserted that digital media are no different than other media, as they serve as a medium for creating art just as paint, drawing, and sculpture do. This perspective represents a stark contrast to the perspective of those in the early 2000s and before, which may be due to researcher bias or simply due to changes in application and perspective in the intervening decade. Additionally, earlier authors refer more to passive consumption of media while later authors speak more of direct engagement with such media. The truth more likely lies in the middle, where there are both benefits and major concerns regarding use of digital media.

Orr (2016), however, asserted that digital art media open possibilities beyond what traditional art media can offer, such as with user-friendly animation and virtual reality. Digital art media allow participants to explore a range of media characteristics (for example, drawing, painting, and sculpting) without requiring direct access to those media—and they provide "an abbreviated version of the whole psyche" (Thong 2007, p.58). Visual technology (such as online image searches) has expanded the availability of source material for artwork, and programs like Photoshop have opened up what participants can do with the images they gather (Henley 2018), providing instant gratification and inspiration for finding and sharing desired images.

Positive influence of popular culture and digital technology in the art therapy space

Potash (2009) examined the potential positive effects of popular media in art therapy with adolescents through the transformation of popular images into personally meaningful images, but he also acknowledged that the instant gratification and passivity encouraged by popular culture and media can damage client interactions and social skills, citing examples from his own practice. Digital media promote an instantaneous, often visual, omnipresent popular/consumer culture, which has both good and bad sides (Orr, 2010). Potash reasoned that, "given the power of images, art therapists may be in a unique position to examine the impact of pop culture on adolescents and explore ways to mitigate it, if necessary" (2009, p.52). This claim presupposes that the art produced in therapy provides similar metaphorical and distancing experiences as popular media, but that the presence of an empathizing adult, the art therapist, and the creation of an art image assist in creating therapeutic change. Potash referenced Dunn-Snow (1993) as being among the first to examine the potential positive influence of popular media when therapists work with children in her example of *Teenage Mutant Ninja Turtles* as a metaphor for confronting thoughts and feelings "experienced in the course of growing up" (p.102). Art therapists can harness the constant bombardment of visual culture (Orr, 2010), putting to use the metaphors that Potash and Dunn-Snow recognized.

Austin (2009) also saw the art therapy session as a space where this content could be worked through, although in his perspective, computer media is fully therapeutic as art media. Although different from traditional art media, the interaction of a client with digital media still has the potential to provide opportunities that are not possible by traditional means alone. Like Potash (2009), Austin asserted that because art therapists are proficient in metaphor and fantasy, they may be more equipped to deal with the potential impacts of technology, such as processing violent images. However, Austin suggested that art therapists go beyond facilitating the use of the imagery to create digital art and process conflicts related to digital media exposure.

Reviewing the literature, which only began in the first decade of the 21st century to examine digital technology impacts on art therapy, I reflected that I was trained in art therapy around the same time, in 2005. I am a digital native and have used a computer in some fashion for nearly as long as I can remember. I have witnessed a disparity generationally among many art therapists, which is to be expected, although some of my peers did not have the early computer exposure I had. I have also observed that those who grew up without this exposure are much more resistant to technology integration than I am. Compared to 10 years ago, current students are much more likely to be comfortable with digital media and have a desire to integrate digital media into their practice. My current child and adolescent participants also warm up to me quickly when I encourage them to share their favorite video game or YouTube video with me. Perhaps, as Orr (2010) reasoned, digital media now are ubiquitous, and so many people integrate these media into their personal identity: gamer, programmer, YouTuber, etc. If a therapist recognizes and validates these identities, it can assist in developing relationships with participants.

More recently, art therapists have encouraged the use of video games and films, or their content, within the therapy session.

Brown and Garner (2017) reported that video games in therapy can break down resistance for adolescents, and argued that video gaming is "artistic expression" (p.193), although the level of artistic expression is dependent on the type of video game. In working with autistic individuals, I have also used video games in therapy sessions, and found that offering the space to discuss the games can be therapeutic for participants. For example, one child liked to play "Bendy and the Ink Machine" (2008), a horror video game with many jump scares. Playing this game in session afforded opportunities for problem-solving, discussing ways to work through aggression other than physical violence, and even practicing social skills, as when a child engages in doing a voice for the main character and the therapist voices a side character.

POPULAR MEDIA AND CULTURE IN ART THERAPY WITH INDIVIDUALS WITH AUTISM

Humburg and Wolf Bordonaro (2017) and Wolf Bordonaro, Stallings, and Humburg (2017) described the use of popular film in art therapy with individuals on the autism spectrum. Humburg (2016) developed a directive guide targeting the areas articulated by Betts *et al.* (2014) to include cognitive growth, emotional regulation, adaptive behavioral styles, and physical development as possible goals for interventions based on popular films. Van Lith, Stallings, Harris, and Campbell (2017) detailed implementation of an eight-session group intervention for individuals with autism, describing a case where one participant centered his art expression on the character Oh from the movie *Home*. Utilizing this character appeared to increase the participant's comfort in the group and assist him in relating to his peers.

Although in his earlier work he emphasized the problems technology could cause participants (Kramer *et al.* 1997), Henley (2018) has since accepted the need for art therapists to adapt to cultural trends, and noted that the pervasiveness of digital technology in participants' and therapists' lives goes far beyond anything he could have ever predicted. He asserted that video games and TV problematically normalize aggression and violence, but also contended that art therapists can offer a holding space in which to work through this material. He emphasized the importance of parental and therapist engagement and guidance to ensure safety and continued social engagement as well as prevention of addictive behavior and disconnection from reality.

Henley (2018) recognized both positive and negative aspects in gaming and social media, noted by art therapists and non-art therapists alike. He acknowledged the potential for talking about and imitating video games and other pop-culture media in providing an avenue for social connection: "With such tools at their disposal, technology has given children on the spectrum potentially a new and forceful voice" (Henley 2018, p.155). He also pointed out these topics as ways to build therapeutic rapport with individuals with autism, and reported that he does so by showing benign interest in an individual's cultural interests (for example, anime characters or video games) to build the relationship. He did not encourage artwork focusing on these topics, but did not discourage it. He cautioned that the inclusion of technology in session can both increase and decrease creativity and must be monitored and shaped by the art therapist, such as encouraging a client to come up with original stories about preferred characters rather than perseverating on drawing one pre-existing scene.

Henley (2018) recognized that most autistic children absorb "the 'visual culture' that surrounds" them (p.161). Autistic individuals create their own meaning for these images amidst their obsessions, as Potash (2009) identified with neurotypical teenagers. This absorption of visual culture may provide neurodivergent individuals "an advantage in the future" (Henley 2018, p.162). There is thus some support in the literature for digital technology providing an extension of the self and a sense of safety for individuals with autism. Media such as cameras and smartphones may offer a gateway to artistic creation as well as a distance from environments that are overwhelming or uncomfortable, which can be put to creative use in art therapy, for example by helping a client practice a social situation by interacting with a picture of it.

Henley (2018) theorized that electronics such as smartphones may provide a kind of "symbiotic" relationship with autistic participants providing opportunities to build relationships in the therapy setting through use of technology as a transitional space. Art therapists can help assist navigation of this transitional space. I have frequently done so by asking participants with autism to draw problems or issues they are having and then substitute their favorite popular culture figures, which provides a metaphorical distance for working through the situation. Relatedly, Henley (2018) recognized that many individuals with autism identify with powerful characters that provide feelings of power and protection.

IMPLICATIONS FOR ART THERAPY PRACTICE

It is important to note that too much time using technology-based interests can lead to sleep disruptions, over-stimulation, increased social difficulties, increased anxiety, shortened attention span, and addiction to screen-based technologies (Dunckley 2015). Similar to Henley (2018), in my experience, integrating these interests into the therapy session and/or adapting these interests into art and play-based activities can help in addressing these concerns. The art therapist can shape this identification with popular media therapeutically. In my experience this engagement of client interests, especially through digital media, encourages client agency and investment in the art therapy session and builds the therapeutic relationship.

Based in the literature and clinical experience shared in Part One, Part Two of this book will describe and explore the special interest communication theory (SICT) and provide examples to use as a framework in therapeutic practice. The case examples are case composites based on years of working with autistic children, teens, and young adults. None of the participants mentioned represent a single person but are instead composed from characteristics I often observed. All participants are presented as gender-neutral.

Part Two

CHAPTER 6

Special Interest Communication Theory (SICT) Facilitative Framework

The largest bodies of research regarding therapies associated with autism, such as ABA and CBT, suggest that highly structured and short-term therapies are efficacious. These therapies overtly decline to focus on, and at times inadvertently discount, participants' emotional needs and specific desires. In my experience, autistic individuals may benefit more from metaphorical approaches because they already excel in concrete and linear thinking (as this is a primary characteristic of autism), and often desire practice in open-ended, ambiguous kinds of interaction. Metaphorical approaches encourage interaction in new ways, such as having a dialogue with a participant's favorite video game character to encourage social and emotional practice. Also, an artistic metaphorical approach arguably makes concepts more concrete or linear for participants by providing visual material to address in therapy. Furthermore, the child-centered play therapy (CCPT) literature indicates that a less structured participant-led approach to therapy is often successful with autistic children. CCPT argues that following the participant's lead in building the therapeutic relationship is what makes less structured approaches successful and encourages addressing emotional needs. It is with this knowledge and my clinical experience (examples provided in the following case examples) that I chose to explore and develop the special interest communication theory (SICT) facilitative framework.

CASE EXAMPLES

GEORGIE

Just after the September 11, 2001, attacks, when I was 21 years old, I started working as a lay behavioral therapist, following the strict rules of applied behavior analysis (ABA), to teach a young child, Georgie, skills they needed in order to be ready for school when they turned five. We repeated pattern games and word identification, role-played age-appropriate play as identified by the ABA consultant, and I imitated animal noises in the way many preschoolers do naturally, repeatedly. Georgie received rewards for completing the tasks I asked of them, for imitating my animal noises, for matching the right pictures, and so on. They sometimes seemed anxious, concerned about whether the monster in the attic playroom (where we had our ABA sessions) would get them, but this was beside the point: it was not what I was there to address, even though they sometimes did not appear able to concentrate because of this fear, or sometimes had "tantrums"—crying and throwing themself on the floor—seemingly related to it. Anyway, I was just an undergraduate studying art and psychology who did not know how to address this anxiety, so I did what I was supposed to, redirecting them to the task at hand and offering Goldfish crackers as a reward. Still, I wondered: would it help to be warmer and fuzzier, to offer comfort for this worry? I noticed that reenacting scenes from Dora the Explorer calmed them, so

I encouraged this during our breaks. We concluded our ABA sessions after 16 months.

Georgie loved *Veggie Tales*—they sang the songs, would act out scenes, and loved to watch the videos. I wondered if there was a way to use *Veggie Tales* as more than just a reward. I continued to contemplate this through three post-baccalaureate degrees and years of practice. I found my practice evolving over the years to embrace these interests and how they could function in the therapeutic relationship while prioritizing the desires and goals of the person with autism.

I noticed similar underlying anxiety to Georgie's over the years when working with individuals of all ages diagnosed with autism. The anxiety might be about an intruder drill coming up at school (the anticipation of the alarm almost too much to bear), not being able to make friends in the same way as peers, a break in routine like an unanticipated snow day, a subject that was just too hard at school, not being able to hold a job because of not being able to quite figure out what a boss wants, or really anything that many neurotypicals often also experience as anxiety provoking. The difference came in how my participants would react. Whereas many neurotypicals might talk to someone about how they felt, assess how they might change the situation, seek comfort in a hug from a person close to them, or go to their doctor and ask if medication might help, my participants would often experience meltdowns, becoming inconsolable with heaving sobs and/or screams or violent tantrums, hitting and kicking and throwing themselves or objects on the floor (although rarely hurting or attempting to hurt others). Another difference I noticed was how most teachers and clinicians and other professionals addressed this anxiety. They saw it as behavioral defiance and often ignored the person's emotional health, and punished these meltdowns without trying to find the cause.

JAMIE

Fast forward a few years and I am working as a counselor and art therapist with Jamie. Jamie is small—not smaller than one would expect for their age, but they look a little crouched next to their mother, where they hide their face, turned away from me. They are nine years old and recently diagnosed with autism. They qualify for a diagnosis that the doctors and clinicians in their life call Level 1, meaning that to many they appear typical most of the time: academically proficient, friendly (most of the time), but quiet. Although capable of doing their schoolwork, they would rather watch YouTube, so in that respect they are not very different from most of their peers in the US in the 2010s. Where they are noticeably different is when they throw what outsiders see as "tantrums," sort of like those of a two- or three-year-old. When Jamie gets angry they throw things, charge people, hit, kick, and knock their younger siblings over. It is as though they are unable to control their actions or ask for help. They first got on the radar of the local mental health center when they lunged at a peer at Sunday school, giving the child a bruise on their arm. When people do not know Jamie, many see them as a child who lacks discipline, a child whose parents disengage and are unwilling to punish or set boundaries. This is not what I see, and certainly not what Jamie's parents are like.

I quickly observe apparent anxiety in Jamie. Their anxiety has many roots: the adoption of their youngest sibling, the illness that sometimes puts their father in hospital, their peers refusing to always do what they want to do at recess, having to share their beloved iPad with their older sister, their concern that a tornado might take them away, my computer failing to load a program, and so on. How do I know this is anxiety and not just signs of what others might see as a spoiled and defiant child? Jamie's anxiety is betrayed by their inability to be distracted by anything else, their insistence in the moment that the world is ending (although not expressed in so many words), their refusal to talk about what is happening, and their inability to self-soothe (which some read as refusal to do so)—this is different. Sure, these patterns appear in other kids, but in my experience neurotypical kids self-soothe or seek soothing from others 9 times out of 10, especially once they attain school age. Kids and adults with autism or other neurodivergent ways of interacting with the world struggle to do so, which is then often made worse by being punished for what is perceived as defiant behavior but may, in reality, be an anxiety attack or generalized anxiety.

Jamie is generally friendly once they know you. However, when I first met them they clung to their mother, more like a toddler than a typical nine-year-old, and they often mumbled "I don't like you" or even "Fuck you" under their breath when I would try to talk to them. It took a couple of months for them to warm to me and allow me to see them without their mother present. We bonded over YouTube. They shared fan-made videos with me based on popular cartoons and video games. They had a particular penchant for internet-based games like "Minecraft," and for catchy little videos like *Nyan Cat*, which some people have compiled versions of that repeat for more than 10 hours. Jamie would be content to watch recordings of "YouTubers" playing "Minecraft" for hours, if I would let him. They felt much the same way about watching *Nyan Cat*. I was hesitant at first to include these things in our sessions, especially because having to transition away from these preferred activities was often what caused bigger behavioral incidents, such as Jamie leaving the room and walking around the building, refusing to return, or knocking over my lamps and throwing my pillows, or, on rare occasions, attempting to hit me. Was I really doing art therapy if we were just watching people play video games online? Was I causing more harm than good by allowing these things that led to such behavioral outbursts in session?

Figure 1: Nesting doll representation of Jamie

This nesting doll, which I created, represents the therapeutic journey with Jamie, showing Jamie's interests ("Minecraft" and "Five Nights at Freddy's") and finally, Jamie themselves, at the core.

I have learned so much from working with kids like Jamie and Georgie, and wanted to be able to articulate what I had learned and provide practical applications for others. I describe what I learned in this chapter and the chapters ahead with practical tips for use in art therapy, counseling, or even by parents or caregivers at home, to engage in positive and person-centered ways using special interests.

SPECIAL INTEREST COMMUNICATION THEORY (SICT) FACILITATIVE FRAMEWORK

Based on my clinical experience I developed a grounded theory-based study for my dissertation. With the approval of the Mount Mary University Institutional Review Board, I conducted a retrospective review of clinical notes from my private practice from 2011 to 2018. I ultimately reviewed the files of eight participants with autism (six children/adolescents and two adults). Of the 350 notes I reviewed, 187 mentioned popular culture in some form. I categorized these mentions and assessed their functions within the context of the documented therapeutic interactions, which I will discuss later in this chapter. All categorical references to popular culture appeared in the session notes with six participants who ranged in age from 7 to 15 and had diagnoses of either Level 1 or Level 2 autism. In contrast, my session notes with two adult participants (in their twenties and thirties, one with Level 1 autism and one with Level 3 autism) did not include any mentions of popular culture (see Figure 2).

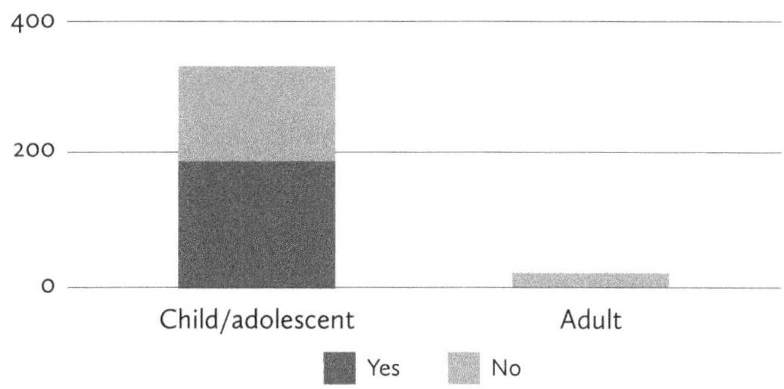

Figure 2: Popular culture references in session notes

This does not necessarily mean that popular culture-based interactions did not occur with the adult participants, but rather that I did not directly document them in my notes, and so their interactions were not available as data in this study. Another relevant point here is that I had no fewer than 30 sessions with each of the participants under 18 years of age, whereas I had an average of only 10 sessions with the participants older than 18. Age and/or number of sessions are variables that may have influenced the content of the sessions. Although these descriptive statistics were unnecessary in grounded theory analysis, calculating them assisted me in assessing whether further exploration of this observation was warranted.

Additionally, I reviewed the footage from a documentary I produced in early 2018 entitled *Art Therapy: The Missing Piece* to identify patterns of popular culture inclusion. Finally, I conducted a video walk-through interview with an 11-year-old diagnosed with autism and reviewed the associated video.

Across these data sources I identified six categories describing how popular culture interests functioned in the art therapeutic relationship forming the special interest communication theory (SICT): (a) behavioral reward; (b) social initiator; (c) social facilitator; (d) personal metaphor; (e) anxiety mediator; and (f) communication clarifier. These six categories form a facilitative framework for conducting art therapy with folks with autism, particularly children, but there is also potential for application with adults.

THE FACILITATIVE FRAMEWORK

As identified in the literature review, art therapists historically have been hesitant to include popular culture elements, especially techno-digital culture artifacts such as video games and YouTube videos, in their practice. This hesitance, or at times resistance, seems to relate to a variety of concerns that include a lack of familiarity with the media (Austin 2009; Brown & Garner 2017; Kapitan 2007; Orr 2005) and subject matter (Henley 2018), and a desire to provide a technology-free space for participants who lead technology-saturated lives (Gerity 2001; Klorer 2009; Kramer 1971; Kramer *et al.* 1997). Reluctance may also be due to limitations of the systems in which art therapists work that may not allow use of video games or computers while in session, or art therapist concerns over repetitive stereotyped imagery. However, ignoring or refusing to include such elements in work with neurodivergent participants may actually delay or impede the development of the therapeutic relationship because of the differences in how neurodivergent individuals think and interact as compared to neurotypical individuals. Support for this claim can be found in research that suggests that special interests are correlated with sensory under- and over-stimulation (Liss *et al.* 2006), and provide the participant with a way to cope with these uncomfortable sensory feelings. Research also suggests that engaging special interests in social situations increases social motivation (Boyd *et al.* 2007; Vismara & Lyons 2007).

These and other research studies indicate that engaging with autistic participants through their special interests is advantageous in therapy. My research also supports this claim. If an art therapist can create a bridge to neurodivergent participants' realities by showing interest in their special interests rather than requiring them to show interest in art materials and topics they may lack a natural interest in, the relationship is likely to develop more quickly and on the participant's own terms. Popular culture elements thus facilitate the relationship and assist in meeting therapeutic goals. Although this framework is built specifically on work with autistic folks, it stands to reason that any relationship can be built better when the therapist shows interest in the participant's interests!

This facilitative framework is not a step-by-step therapeutic process. Rather, SICT is a recursive framework—parts of the framework may be revisited frequently while other parts are not used at all. The framework is composed of six themes, discussed below. Each theme is elaborated on in the following chapters, and several strategies for working with that theme in practice are also included in each chapter that follows. Above all, it is more important to follow the therapy participant's lead and provide an autism positive environment.

Popular culture as behavioral reward

Popular culture may be used as a reward in therapy to encourage desired behaviors and participation in therapy. This may include practices such as watching YouTube and playing video games at the end of a session or offering small prizes such as themed stickers or trading cards. I provide further examples of this in Chapter 7.

Popular culture as social initiator

Sharing of popular culture and other special interests can help to initiate social relationships. Generally, in therapy this involves participants sharing their interest/preferred topics with the therapist, although it may also occur in reverse. In my experience a therapist's willingness to share and geek out on topics can facilitate progress in therapy. For example, my participants and I often share favorite YouTube videos, co-participate in video games, or co-create or simultaneously create artwork based on our popular culture and other special interests. I elaborate on this in Chapter 8.

Popular culture as social facilitator

Popular culture and other special interests can serve as a social buffer for addressing uncomfortable topics. Topics such as traumatic experiences, grief, and getting into trouble are often easier to address through creating artwork and comic strips about preferred characters having similar experiences. Additionally, preferred characters can serve as surrogates for participants in identifying and processing emotions and developing coping skills by identifying examples in the characters' stories or creating new stories for the characters. This typically involves acting out or creating art about specific scenarios that have occurred in the life of the participant, such as acting out a fight with a family member through use of preferred characters. I provide further examples in Chapter 9.

Popular culture as personal metaphor

Related to but distinct from popular culture/special interests as social facilitator, I noticed these interests were often developed into personal metaphors. This theme involves a deeper processing of the material, creating more general and metaphorical situations related to what they are processing as a therapy participant, such as using a tornado to symbolize strong feelings or a video game scenario such as “Grand Theft Auto” to describe their trauma history. As therapists we can encourage the development of these stereotypical themes into personalized metaphors. See Chapter 10 for more information.

Popular culture as anxiety mediator

I observed that the autistic children I worked with often participated in popular culture special interest-based interactions while processing anxiety or immediately after. Special interests may be used as coping/distress tolerance skills while processing or as preparation for processing anxiety, for example processing anxiety over an upcoming surgery while drawing dissections of robots from a favorite video game. You can find further examples in Chapter 11.

Popular culture as communication clarifier

Describing incidents from movies, TV, and video games can help participants convey understanding of a situation or concept, or assist participants in explaining situations or perspectives. The most salient example for me was when a child participant created a set of characters representing themself, my intern, and myself. The child then had their character engage in destructive behavior, destroying a collaboratively built town. Following that they sent their character to therapy with our characters, and declared they would no longer be destructive, illustrating that they understood at least on some level the purpose of the therapeutic relationship. This and other examples are elaborated on in Chapter 12.

TREATMENT PLANNING AND DOCUMENTATION

It can be hard to articulate treatment plans and documentation in ways that managed care agencies approve when your notes reflect repeated drawings of tornadoes sweeping away video game characters and YouTubers, and there is little in “measurable behavior change" to the standards that managed care upholds for extended periods. So, I had to figure out how to create goals and objectives as well as progress in ways that fit what insurance companies desired. Tips for doing so are included in each of the following chapters. There is repetition of goals as well as similar or repeated case studies when such examples represent more than one theme.

CONCLUSION

Taken together, these findings offer a SICT facilitative framework for how popular culture and other special interests may be employed in art therapy as a way to facilitate the therapeutic relationship and therapeutic progress while considering the preferences and interests of the autistic art therapy participants. Encouraging expression through imagery and creative practices with which the participant is comfortable, rather than dismissing such imagery as stereotypical, facilitates relationship building and progress in art therapy. Similarly, allowing and even encouraging playing video games or watching YouTube videos together can also assist in building therapeutic rapport and facilitating therapeutic progress. Therapists can encourage participants to identify positive aspects of their autism identity and their personal goals while working with any of the identified themes. I provide examples of how in the chapters ahead.

CHAPTER 7

Popular Culture as Behavioral Reward

As described in Chapter 6, popular culture may be used as a reward in therapy to encourage desired behaviors and participation in therapy. These rewards may include playing games, watching videos, and earning small prizes like stickers, trading cards, or small toys. However, it is important to distinguish this practice from more traditional behavioral therapies such as ABA. In traditional ABA these rewards are provided for performing behaviors generally defined by non-autistic adults or parents/caregivers. As detailed in Part One of this book, too much focus on changing the autistic person can lead to suicidal feelings and actions and poor self-esteem. When using "rewards" here, I am instead referring to achieving goals that the participant has set for themself, and participation in addressing emotional needs through therapy. Additionally, rewards in this context may be for avoiding harmful behaviors or for participating in self-selected, adaptive coping skills.

CASE EXAMPLES, TREATMENT PLANNING AND DOCUMENTATION

JAMIE, CONTINUED

Jamie responded to offers of paper and marker. They liked to draw their preferred video characters in addition to watching them. This made me feel a little better about using the videos in session; we could bargain—draw first, video later—or make a drawing of the video they liked, which I could usually parlay into making art focused on their interests. Jamie also liked Thomas the Tank Engine. We drew trains together, I taught them one point perspective, even though they were a bit young for it. I encouraged Jamie to lead where the art went and asked a few questions, verbally or visually, related to what the school and their parents reported as areas of difficulty for Jamie, to encourage Jamie to share with me what they saw as in need of change and what caused them distress/whether or not they agreed with the adults' assessment. Although their initial goals were set by their parents due to their age, building our relationship in this way helped Jamie to explore their personal goals. We concluded sessions by playing video games or watching YouTube.

Goal

Jamie and the therapist will build therapeutic rapport through exploring Jamie's interests, as evidenced by Jamie's continued engagement in the therapy process, per documentation.

Objective

Jamie will identify what they would like to focus on in therapy independent of what has been identified by the adults.

Interventions:

- The clinician will encourage Jamie to share their likes and dislikes through art and play, as evidenced in the documentation.

- The clinician will encourage Jamie to identify things they would like to change in their life through art and play, as evidenced in session documentation.

Sample note

The clinician used a person-centered approach to encourage Jamie to share about their likes and dislikes. Jamie shared that they like the *Nyan Cat* video, and shared it with the clinician on YouTube. Jamie created an image of the character Nyan Cat and said that Nyan Cat doesn't like it when the music is too loud. Jamie said that they want to find ways to not feel bad when they hear loud noises. The clinician encouraged Jamie to identify ways they and Nyan Cat could ask for help and help themselves when there are loud noises. The clinician also stated that she would work with Jamie's teacher and parents so they can help with making things quieter. After Jamie and the clinician made a plan to help Jamie with loud noises, the clinician provided an iPad for Jamie to play "Minecraft" for the last few minutes of the session.

PEYTON

Peyton was an eight-year-old child at the time of this session. Peyton was adopted into a large family while in kindergarten and had experienced many losses related to their birth family, as well as a significant amount of trauma related to early childhood abuse and neglect. On this occasion, Peyton's parents had reported that Peyton was sad about the death of their great-aunt and was also having difficulty leaving the house due to their fear of bees. I encouraged Peyton to share about their great-aunt and to work on a plan for coping with their fear of bees. After participating in the session Peyton was rewarded with time playing on a train simulator app on my iPad.

Goal

Peyton will increase their understanding of grief and loss, as evidenced by assessment and self-report.

Objective

Peyton will engage in grief-processing education and activities.

Interventions:

- The clinician will introduce psychoeducation materials and activities related to understanding and processing grief, as evidenced in the documentation.
- Peyton will receive a reward for participation in session that Peyton has selected at the beginning of the session, as evidenced in the documentation.

Goal

Peyton will apply adaptive coping skills and reduce their anxiety, as evidenced by assessment, self-report, and session documentation.

Objective

Peyton will identify and practice coping skills to utilize when experiencing anxiety.

Interventions:

- The clinician will encourage Peyton to draw and share about anxiety, as evidenced in the documentation.
- The clinician will provide psychoeducation about coping skills and engage Peyton in identifying and practicing coping skills they would like to try when anxious, as evidenced in the documentation.
- Peyton will receive a reward for participation in session that Peyton has selected at the beginning of the session, as evidenced in the documentation.

Note: the special interests don't always have to be directly referenced in the goals and interventions.

Sample note

Peyton engaged in psychoeducation worksheets about grief and phobias. Peyton created an illustration about their feelings of fear and sadness when provided with art materials to use. Peyton shared the image with the clinician and the clinician provided validation of their feelings. The clinician encouraged Peyton to add a coping skill to their emotions image, and Peyton did so. At the end of the session the clinician provided Peyton 10 minutes of time on the train simulator on the iPad. [If this was an actual therapy note, copies of the psychoeducational materials and art would be attached.]

STEVIE

Stevie was a young high schooler when they first started seeing me for art therapy. They experienced social anxiety and phobia of storms that made it difficult for them to leave the house. Stevie expressed a desire to develop coping skills that would help with their anxiety, although they were also hesitant to share about them. Stevie and I agreed that they would earn a hot wheel or similar car at the end of the session, after processing anxieties and practicing coping skills.

Goal

Stevie stated a desire to apply adaptive coping skills and reduce their anxiety response; progress will be evidenced by assessment, self-report, and session documentation.

Objective

Stevie will identify and practice coping skills to utilize when experiencing anxiety.

Interventions:

- The clinician will encourage Stevie to create imagery/artwork and share about their anxiety, as evidenced in the documentation.
- The clinician and Stevie will research storms and statistics about lethality as well as safety, per Stevie's request.
- The clinician will provide psychoeducation about coping skills and engage Stevie in identifying and practicing coping skills they would like to try, as evidenced in the documentation.
- Stevie will receive a reward for participation in session that Stevie has selected at the beginning of the session, as evidenced in the documentation.

Sample note

At the beginning of the session the clinician provided Stevie with two toy cars to pick from for session reward. Stevie and the clinician then used the clinician's laptop to research storms and their frequency in the region. The clinician offered a choice of creating a picture-based story about storms or creating a storm survival kit. The clinician provided supplies to design and fill an emergency kit to help with storm safety, and Stevie stated they would like to complete this project this day. Stevie made their kit and also made a list of additional supplies they would place in it when they arrived home. At the end of the session the clinician gave Stevie their toy car reward.

ALEX

Alex was a middle-schooler whom I had seen in a school setting for several months. Alex had difficulty with aggressive outbursts or leaving the classroom without permission when experiencing sensory overload or frustration. Alex had used sticker charts in a previous setting to earn rewards. Alex requested a sticker chart to help meet their goals of using adaptive coping skills such as fidgets rather than hurting themself or others. Alex worked with me to define things they should earn stickers for, what kind of stickers we should use, what the chart should look like, and what rewards they would like to earn. I engaged Alex in all levels of this process, so they had control over the process and so that the chart did not simply feature demands provided by adults.

Goal

Alex stated a desire to get less angry when experiencing sensory overload or frustration. The clinician will measure progress through self-report, and clinician, parent, and classroom observation.

Objective

Alex will identify anger triggers.

Interventions:

- Alex will participate in identifying anger triggers through behavior chaining after anger incidents.
- The clinician will engage Alex in activities to identify the earliest signs of anger and in making plans for when to apply coping and distractor skills, as evidenced in the documentation.

Objective

Alex also stated they would like to increase associated coping skills. Alex will identify and practice coping strategies.

Interventions:

- The clinician will provide education about coping strategies.
- The clinician will engage Alex in art directives for exploration

of current and future coping skills (such as creating a reward chart).

- The clinician and Alex will practice Alex's coping skills together.

Sample note

In session, while discussing the use of coping skills and coping ahead plans, Alex identified that they would find a reward chart helpful to remind them of their coping skills and what they could earn for successful application. The clinician provided positive feedback for this idea, and encouraged Alex to identify skills they wished to use and earn rewards for, to set the frequency of rewards and the types of rewards in collaboration with the clinician and their parents (see, for example, Figure 3, at the end of this chapter).

CAL

Cal was a young adult when they presented for sessions with me. They identified a desire to communicate better with family and friends, and to reduce their overall social anxiety, but more specifically as it applied to dating and romantic relationships. These were generally the themes of our sessions. Cal liked to make jewelry and was an expert in techniques that I was not versed in; at the end of sessions Cal would take over and instruct me in these jewelry-making methods. Additionally, we talked about our favorite sci-fi fantasy shows at the end of session, a favorite genre of Cal's.

Goal

Cal articulated a desire to improve their communication skills and reduce their social anxiety. Progress will be measured through self-report and structured assessment of their social anxiety symptoms.

Objective

Assess specific areas of communication on which Cal would like to work.

Interventions:

- The clinician will engage Cal in communication-style assessments to help identify areas Cal feels are in need of development.
- The clinician will engage Cal in creation of comic strips/graphic novellas to identify situations where Cal felt they could improve in their communication skills.
- The clinician will engage Cal in developing more specific goals for communication and update their treatment plan.

Objective

Assess symptoms of social anxiety on which Cal would like to work, and develop coping strategies for said anxiety.

Interventions:

- The clinician will engage Cal in social anxiety assessments to further identify anxiety symptoms.
- The clinician will engage Cal in art-directed interventions and semi-structured interviews to explore situations where their anxiety is highest.
- Cal will participate in identifying anxiety triggers through behavior chaining after anxiety incidents; this behavior chaining will be attached to session notes.
- The clinician will engage Cal in art directives for exploration of current and future coping skills.

Sample note

Cal identified an incident where they had experienced conflict with their mother. Cal shared that their mother had confronted them about content they watched on YouTube. Cal expressed a desire to handle the situation differently the next time, and the clinician encouraged them to make an image of how they handled it this time and how they wanted to handle it the next time. Cal quickly did so using the anime style that they preferred. Following this Cal decided they would like to ask their mother clarifying questions about what she didn't like about YouTube, and also to take their prescribed as needed medication (PRN) earlier in the exchange to help them to handle the situation differently. With the clinician they explored a list of questions and then participated in a brief body mapping exercise, again, in anime style, to identify physical signs of anxiety that could help cue them to take their medication earlier. At the end of session the clinician encouraged Cal to teach her a new jewelry technique that they had expressed excitement about earlier in the session as a means to return to equilibrium after discussing and creating about a difficult topic. Cal showed the clinician the basic steps and the clinician and Cal agreed to finish the jewelry out of session to share with each other next time.

TREATMENT APPLICATIONS/ACTIVITIES

- When beginning the therapeutic relationship, encourage the participant to share with you what makes them happy, what they enjoy doing in their free time, what they like to tell others about, and what their personal goals (therapeutic or otherwise, to help shape the treatment plan) are, and have them select what they would like to use as rewards for participation in sessions.
- Encourage introductory artwork, introducing themselves and

their preferences. Co-participate in this—participants often want to know more about us, and willingness to share small things goes a long way:

  - Mutually share clips from preferred shows, movies, YouTube videos, etc.
  - Play video games together in initial sessions as part of the rapport-building process.
  - Provide coloring sheets from preferred topics for use while performing verbal/written assessments or for in-between art-based assessments.

- Integrating rewards:
  - Set aside 15 minutes at the end of the session to play video games together.
  - Print coloring pages of preferred media and provide them as a reward at the end of the session.
  - Stock up on stickers representing the participant's interests.
  - Watch a movie in short segments over several sessions.
  - Shift the topic to preferred interests for the last 15 minutes or so of the session.
- If the participant wants to utilize a reward chart, engage them in making one:
  - For these reward charts have the participant define what they will earn stickers or stamps for, and how many stickers or stamps they will need to earn to get a larger reward—you may need them to define levels of rewards such as small, medium, and large, which can take different amounts of stickers to earn (see Figure 3, for example).

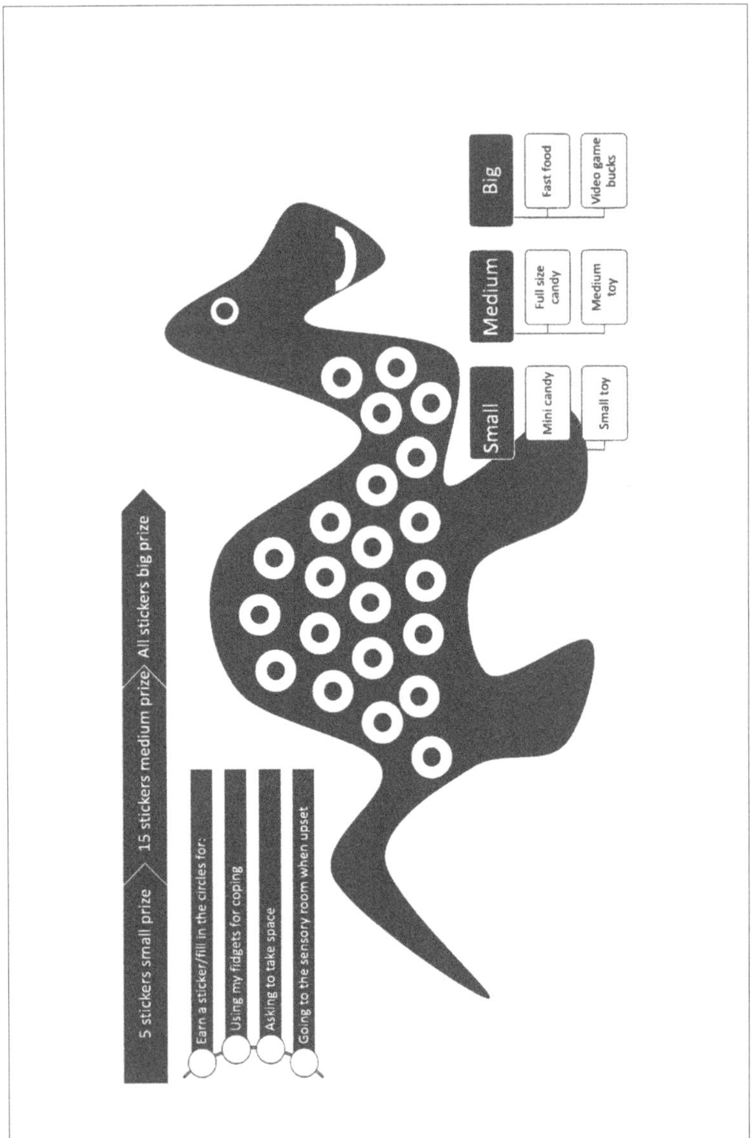

Figure 3: Sample reward chart made with PowerPoint by the author

CHAPTER 8

Popular Culture as Social Initiator

Sharing of popular culture and other special interests can help to initiate social relationships. Usually this involves participants sharing about their interests and preferences (some of the elements of implementation overlap with learning preferences of the participant for purposes of rewards); however, the clinician may also share some of their interests and preferences as part of rapport building. As I stated previously, in my experience, the willingness of therapists to share and geek out on topics can facilitate progress in therapy. For example, I often share with my participants favorite YouTube videos, co-participate in video games, or co-create or create simultaneously artwork based on our popular culture and other special interests.

CASE EXAMPLES, TREATMENT PLANNING AND DOCUMENTATION

JAMIE, CONTINUED

Jamie initially declined to address any of the concerns their parents mentioned, like anger outbursts, aggression toward their adopted sibling, or their reported difficulty socializing with peers. I continued to encourage Jamie to share their favorite YouTube videos, and we watched many of Jamie's favorite cartoons and YouTubers.

I shared with Jamie "The Hamster Dance" that was popular on the early internet when I was younger. As Jamie became more comfortable with me, I could ask them to draw pictures of the video game characters or YouTubers they liked experiencing scenarios like those that were happening in their life, or with the help of my intern, role-play these things with Thomas toys and other figurines. Jamie confided in me that their occasional under-the-breath cursing was from reading YouTube comments and watching YouTubers that their parents had forbidden while unsupervised.

Note: the goal, objective, and interventions are repeated from Chapter 7, as they are still applicable here.

Goal

Jamie and the clinician will build therapeutic rapport through exploring Jamie's interests, as evidenced by Jamie's continued engagement in the therapy process, per documentation.

Objective

Jamie will identify what they would like to focus on in therapy independent of what has been identified by the adults.

Interventions:

- The clinician will encourage Jamie to share likes and dislikes through art and play, as evidenced in the documentation.
- The clinician will encourage Jamie to identify things they would like to change in their life through art and play, as evidenced in session documentation.

Sample note

Jamie continued to be disinterested in talking about conflict with their sibling and peers. The clinician continued to build a welcoming/person-centered space by encouraging Jamie to share their more favorite YouTube videos. Jamie shared one showing two of their favorite "Minecraft" YouTubers building a world. The clinician also shared a video. The clinician asked Jamie how the two YouTubers would handle a fight over supplies, and Jamie asked for a marker and paper to draw this. When Jamie finished the drawing the clinician asked if things like that ever happened with Jamie and their sibling, and Jamie stated that they did. Jamie reported that they fight with their sibling over their tablet, which can lead to Jamie getting into trouble. Jamie stated they didn't like it when that happened. The clinician encouraged Jamie to identify how they could handle the situation differently. Jamie stated that they were unsure, and didn't want to talk about it anymore. The clinician thanked Jamie and offered her iPad for Jamie to play "Minecraft."

TOMMIE

Tommie was a middle-schooler with a co-occurring diagnosis of selective mutism and a history of significant and ongoing trauma. Tommie would not verbally speak to me in session, and did not do so for the duration of our working relationship. However, I could engage Tommie in play. Tommie liked superheroes. Tommie would co-participate with me in putting together superhero LEGO® sets. The first time I noticed this was when I asked Tommie to show me their favorite superhero at an in-home session. Tommie went to their room and grabbed a bag, brought it to me, and began rummaging through it. Once they found Thor, they pulled it out and handed it to me. I thanked Tommie and shared that I liked Thor too. Tommie later sat side by side with me and we each assembled the same Marvel superheroes LEGO® sets. In another session Tommie drew their favorite video game characters to introduce themself to a new intern who was observing the session. I discontinued working with Tommie when I moved out of state. Tommie continued work with a play therapist (as there wasn't an art therapist available) who was prepared to continue working nonverbally with Tommie.

Goal

Tommie will experience a reduction in anxiety that will increase their ability to participate in daily activities such as school and peer play, as desired. Progress will be assessed through ongoing assessments, clinician observation, and self-report.

Objective

The clinician and Tommie will develop a working relationship where the participant feels safe to share their thoughts and feelings.

Interventions:

- The clinician will actively build trust with Tommie through introducing preferred activities and co-engaging in said activities, as evidenced in the documentation.
- The clinician will speak with Tommie without expectation of response, explaining to Tommie the therapeutic process, and inviting Tommie to continue art and play-based engagement, as evidenced in the documentation.

Note: in a complicated case such as Tommie's, it is recommended working with a speech language pathologist who has additional training in working with individuals with selective mutism.

Sample note

Tommie did not interact with the clinician verbally in this session. Tommie did share their favorite superhero when asked by the clinician to do so, by going to their room and finding the toy and giving it to the clinician to see, as a means of answering the question. Tommie also agreed to work on a LEGO® project with the clinician and sat with the clinician for 30 minutes doing so, which was a longer time period than the previous week, where they had spent 20 minutes with the clinician. The clinician will continue engaging Tommie with preferred toys and providing verbal minimal encouragers and psychoeducation as needed in session.

JAYLIN

Jaylin was a recent high school graduate. Jaylin reported they had diagnoses of autism, disruptive mood dysregulation disorder, as well as relevant trauma history, and a history of verbal and physical aggression. Jaylin reported a desire to better control their anger. Jaylin shared that they liked to draw anime characters and were interested in reducing their anger, but noted that they found it difficult to speak about their anger directly. I encouraged them to share about their favorite anime and to share previously created artwork as a means to build our relationship and increase their comfort in sharing with me.

Goal

Jaylin will develop an awareness of anger triggers and associated thoughts and feelings, and how Jaylin acts on said thoughts/feelings, and identify alternative responses, as evidenced by self-report and clinician documentation.

Objective

Identify anger triggers and common anger responses.

Interventions:

- The clinician will develop a level of trust with Jaylin; provide support and empathy to encourage them to feel safe in expressing anger through encouraging exploration of interests/sharing preferred activities, as evidenced in the documentation.
- Jaylin will create imagery associated with anger triggers and modify that imagery to identify and practice coping skills, as evidenced by photographic documentation attached to session notes.
- Jaylin will practice selected coping skills in session and create a coping kit with the clinician, as evidenced in the documentation.

Sample note

Jaylin actively engaged in the session. The clinician encouraged Jaylin to share about their likes and dislikes and hobbies. Jaylin shared the pictures they had created in their sketchbook prior to the session. Jaylin stated that they liked to draw in anime and manga style, and found that drawing was a way they got their feelings out. Jaylin also shared about their favorite anime shows. When asked by the clinician, Jaylin shared that they identified with two of the characters that were anti-heroes, stating that they identified with being a good person who made mistakes.

TREATMENT APPLICATIONS/ACTIVITIES

- Center the sessions around the participant's preferred interests.
- Encourage introductory artwork, introducing themselves and their preferences. Co-participate in this—participants often want to know more about us, and willingness to share small things goes a long way:
    - Mutually share clips from preferred shows, movies, and videos.
    - Play video games together in initial sessions as part of a rapport-building process.
    - Provide coloring sheets from preferred topics for use while performing verbal/written assessments or for in-between art-based assessments.
    - Don't be afraid to share your experience or lack of experience with their preferences; encourage them to teach you about their preferences.
    - Don't be afraid to share your preferences as well (to a point, as appropriate with specific participants).

- Targeted art directives:
  - Encourage creating artwork representing self as a preferred anime character, sports figure, superhero, or other pop-culture figure.
  - Adapt activities and initial assessments, such as Kinetic Family Drawing, by encouraging use of preferred interests (such as draw your family doing something together such as Pokémon) to encourage engagement and investment.
  - Provide blank comic strips or blank books that are comic formatted for creating personalized comic books; encourage the participant to create a comic or graphic novel introducing themselves and their likes/dislikes/hobbies/self-identified problems, or whatever is relevant for your setting or your participant's needs.
- Further questions to ask in session:
  - What part of [character, game, show, athlete, etc.] do you identify with?
  - What do you like about [character, game, show, athlete, etc.]?
  - What makes you like that [character, game, show, athlete, etc.]?
  - Does the [character, game, show, athlete, etc.] remind you of anything or anyone?
  - If you could live in a [game, show, etc.], which one would you like to live in? Why?
- Further use commercially available products such as those by Geek Therapy to stimulate discussion (see Chapter 13).

CHAPTER 9

Popular Culture as Social Facilitator

As described in Chapter 6, popular culture and other special interests can serve as a social buffer for addressing uncomfortable topics. Topics such as traumatic experiences, grief, and getting into trouble are often easier to address through creating artwork and comic strips about preferred characters having similar experiences. Additionally, preferred characters can serve as surrogates for participants in identifying and processing emotions and developing coping skills by identifying examples in the characters' stories or creating new stories for the characters. This typically involves acting out/creating specific scenarios that have occurred in the life of the participant, such as acting out a fight with a family member through use of preferred characters.

CASE EXAMPLES, TREATMENT PLANNING AND DOCUMENTATION

JAMIE, CONTINUED

We frequently addressed what Jamie's preferred characters' worries were, how they felt, and what led them to throw things. Sometimes we role-played, wrote, and drew stories seemingly unrelated to what was happening with Jamie. A big tornado would hit Sodor, the fictional island where Thomas lived, and we would have to rescue the trains and other characters. Usually when these disasters occurred there was something happening in Jamie's life that made them anxious: a transition to a new school, the death of a family member, bullying, a new diagnosis of diabetes for Jamie. Jamie did not generally make up their own characters and did not name characters after themself (only occasionally after their sister), even though I could always tell which character was them. They also did not allow me to create or introduce new characters; we had to stick to Jamie's script and play these scenarios out for months at a time. After about a year of focusing on the same video game, they suddenly introduced their own characters modeled after the game, named after their youngest sister, and they allowed my intern (who did magnificent voices) to introduce additional characters. Although it was unusual that Jamie would directly acknowledge the connection to their personal experience, working through their stressors with the characters led to visible reductions in their anxiety, and Jamie's parents reported improved sleep and fewer anger-related meltdowns at home and at school.

Goal

Jamie will experience a reduction in their anxiety as evidenced by structured evaluation, parent/classroom/clinician observation, and self-report.

Objective

Jamie will explore anxiety through role-play and coping skills practice, as evidenced in the documentation.

Intervention:

- The clinician will encourage self-directed play/art making; the clinician will play with Jamie and make suggestions for coping tools in the context of play scenarios, following Jamie's lead.

Goal

Jamie will experience a reduction in feelings of anger, as evidenced by structured evaluation, parent/classroom/clinician observation, and self-report.

Objective

Jamie will explore feelings of anger through role-play and coping skills practice, as evidenced in the documentation.

Intervention:

- The clinician will encourage self-directed play/art making; the clinician will play with Jamie and make suggestions for coping tools in the context of play scenarios, following Jamie's lead.

Sample note

Jamie's mother reported that Jamie had just been diagnosed with diabetes and had been "on edge" since learning of the diagnosis. Jamie asked to play a preferred video game in session. The clinician used a child-centered approach and agreed to play the game. While playing the video game the clinician began to voice a secondary character asking the primary character questions about what was bothering them. Jamie began to answer as said character, stating that the character was sick and was worried they wouldn't get better. The clinician validated the character's feelings and, after finishing the game, the clinician asked Jamie to make a "Get well" card for the character. The clinician encouraged Jamie to include examples of coping skills in the card to suggest for the character to use, and Jamie did so, including an image of a character with headphones on, listening to music. Jamie appeared visibly more relaxed at the end of session, as evidenced by them lying on the couch while waiting for their mother, rather than pacing the room, as they had earlier in the session.

ALEX, CONTINUED

Talking and creating about emotions was difficult for Alex. Once, when Alex came to my office visibly upset, I asked them to create an image of their favorite character feeling calm and feeling angry. Alex preferred not to talk directly about emotions they identified as negative, and was more amenable to address them through preferred characters. When asked more directly about whether Alex experienced these emotions, they stated that they experienced calm, but anger was only on TV.

Goal

Alex will identify feelings and their triggers and practice coping skills when faced with said triggers, as evidenced by structured evaluation, parent/classroom/clinician observation, and self-report.

Objective

Alex will explore feelings of anger through art making, role-play, and coping skills practice, as evidenced in the documentation.

Intervention:

- The clinician will provide directed art activities when needed, and encourage self-directed art and play to explore feelings of anger and coping skills through the use of preferred characters/shows.

Objective

Alex will identify and practice three adaptive coping skills, as evidenced by session notes.

Intervention:

- The clinician will provide psychoeducation regarding coping tools and assist Alex in selecting coping tools that Alex prefers.

Sample note

Alex came to the clinician's office visibly upset, as evidenced by their facial expression and slumped body position. Alex stated they didn't know how they felt when the clinician asked. The clinician engaged Alex in a discussion about their favorite anime. After discussing for several minutes, the clinician asked Alex to create an image of their favorite character when the character was calm and when they were angry. Alex did so. The clinician asked Alex if they ever had these feelings. Alex reported that they experienced calm but that the anger feeling was only on TV. The clinician asked Alex to further identify what helped the character feel calm and what made them feel angry. Alex added images to their drawings to illustrate these soothers and triggers. The clinician asked Alex to identify which soothers and triggers applied to them as well, and they stated that watching YouTube was a soother and that people being loud was a trigger. Alex stated that they wanted to ask to have headphones on to watch YouTube when they were upset, and the clinician agreed to help Alex communicate this to their teacher and parents.

TOMMIE, CONTINUED

Tommie had frequent conflicts with their siblings, as reported by their siblings and mother. As mentioned in Chapter 8, Tommie would not verbally speak to me in session, and did not do so for the duration of our working relationship. However, I could at times engage Tommie in written conversation. On one such occasion, Tommie created images of Thor being blown up by creepers from "Minecraft." On this day, Tommie's younger sibling had broken their favorite Thor toy. I engaged Tommie in a written conversation about this image in the context of reports of conflict by their siblings and mother, and encouraged Tommie to use their artwork to cope with their angry feelings.

Goal

Tommie will identify feelings and their triggers and practice coping skills when faced with said triggers, as evidenced by structured evaluation, parent/classroom/clinician observation, and self-report.

Objective

The clinician and Tommie will develop a working relationship where the participant feels safe to share their thoughts and feelings.

Interventions:

- The clinician will actively build trust with Tommie through introducing preferred activities and co-engaging in said activities, as evidenced in the documentation.
- The clinician will communicate with Tommie in ways that Tommie identifies as safe, as evidenced by observation of Tommie and collaboration with their family and other professionals.

Sample note

When the clinician arrived for the session, Tommie's family reported that there had been sibling conflict that day that included a younger sibling breaking one of Tommie's favorite Thor toys and Tommie hitting the sibling. The clinician asked Tommie to draw a picture of how they felt this day, and they drew a picture of Thor being blown up by creepers from "Minecraft." The clinician wrote a message asking if they ever wanted to blow things up. They wrote "maybe," but crossed it out and wrote "no." The clinician asked out loud which they really felt, and they wrote "maybe." The clinician asked if they thought the right answer was "no" and they wrote "yes." The clinician verbally validated Tommie's feelings regarding this feeling, and reinforced that anger was a common feeling and that it was okay to feel this way.

CAL, CONTINUED

As discussed in Chapter 7, Cal was a young adult when they presented for sessions with me. They identified a desire to communicate better with their family and friends, and to reduce their overall social anxiety. Cal expressed difficulty in identifying others' emotions and body language. They enjoyed the show *The Office*, so we used clips of the show to practice these skills. To provide an autism positive therapy experience, I also encouraged Cal to reframe their notion that they were the only one who could make mistakes in relationships. I encouraged Cal to identify ways in which they had succeeded in communication and instances in which their communication partner had miscommunicated.

Goal

"I want to be better able to identify others' feelings from what they say and do." Progress will be evidenced by clinician observation and Cal's self-report and artwork.

Objective

Cal will practice identifying emotions based on facial expression and body language; progress will be tracked through self-report and clinician observation.

Intervention:

- The clinician will provide video clips and structured discussion/practice based on said clips to assist Cal in practicing emotion identification, as documented in session notes.

Objective

Cal will practice understanding of idioms, similes, metaphors, jokes, and sarcasm; progress will be tracked through self-report and clinician observation.

Intervention:

- The clinician will provide video clips and structured discussion/practice based on said clips to assist Cal in identifying and understanding abstract language/when to ask questions regarding abstract language, as documented in session notes.

Objective

Cal will engage in social practice to encourage generalization of skills learned related to emotion identification/understanding other social communication.

Intervention:

- Cal will practice social scenarios through creating a graphic novel exploring social interactions through use of preferred characters.

Sample note

Cal continued to report conflict with their mother. Cal stated they had a difficult time identifying the signs that their mother was becoming frustrated with them. Cal agreed to participate in psychoeducation and practice to better understand signs of frustration. They and the clinician watched clips from *The Office* to practice identifying signs of frustration. They engaged actively in the psychoeducational activity and practice. The clinician also engaged Cal in making comics about their interactions with their mother. The clinician applied cognitive restructuring and reframing to assist Cal in identifying that others also make mistakes in communication, and that the full burden did not lie with Cal. Cal reported that they understood, and began to engage in planning to invite their mother to future session to address the need for changes in interaction on her part as well.

TREATMENT APPLICATIONS/ACTIVITIES

- Utilize preferred interest as a therapist-directed metaphor for addressing a difficult subject in artwork, for instance for a child with aggressive episodes:
  - For example, create an image of what [character/popular personality] would do if someone hit them.
- Encourage creation of pop-culture-themed art centering on a difficult topic:
  - For example, make an image showing what [character/popular personality] would look like if they felt the way the participant does.
- Play a video game and voice the characters to talk about topics that are difficult for the participant to broach—ask which character(s) they would like to be, and then you can voice others:
  - Ask questions centering on therapy goals/incidents in need of addressing.
  - Encourage the participant to create an image based on this play scenario with their preferred media.
- Utilize toys or figurines of preferred interests, and similarly voice/create stories related to the participant's needs:
  - Ask the participant to create an image from this play scenario on completion of play with preferred art materials.
- Play a preferred board, card, or video game while talking about a non-preferred topic:
  - For example, make up therapy rules for UNO™—for instance, "Every time a red card is played share/draw about anger" (you may ask for examples of characters being angry,

the participant being angry, individuals in the participant's life being angry, etc.).

- Adapt commercially available storytelling games such as Nanofictionary or Rory's Story Cubes:
  - With Nanofictionary, select targeted cards related to a therapeutic focus, allow the participant to choose from them, and then ask the participant to tell or create a story.
  - With Rory's Story Cubes, follow existing rules and/or add participant-specific rules. Existing rules: "To create your story, you can use three dice for the setup, three for the story development, and three for the conclusion" (Rory's Story Cubes 2021).

    Participants start the story with "Once upon a time" and create the rest of the story by elaborating on suggestions given by symbols on the dice.

    Add rules such as: "Identify your main character" (based on the participant's interest) prior to rolling the dice; "Identify the conflict of the story," prior to the dice roll, based on the participant's therapy goals or a problem on which the participant is working. Roll the dice to suggest ways to address these goals in the story or to prompt problem-solving.
  - Draw/make a digital a storyboard detailing the participant's story.
- Construct LEGO® sets themed with preferred topics:
  - Encourage storytelling about what is happening to the characters while building occurs.
  - Further encourage creation of a comic or storyboard to continue development of themes and discussion.

CHAPTER 10

Popular Culture as Personal Metaphor

As discussed in Chapter 6, popular culture as personal metaphor describes the transformation of special interests into symbols of personally significant feelings, situations, or representations of therapeutic processing. Unlike popular culture as social facilitator, this theme involves a deeper processing of the material, creating more general and metaphorical situations related to what the therapy participant is processing, such as using a tornado to symbolize strong feelings or a video game scenario such as "Grand Theft Auto" to describe their trauma history. As therapists we can encourage this metaphor development using what may have traditionally been mistaken for stereotypical themes in artwork. In approaching interests in this way, we can work with therapy participants to utilize these metaphors to resolve conflict through role-play and art making.

CASE EXAMPLES, TREATMENT PLANNING AND DOCUMENTATION

JAMIE, CONTINUED

Once Jamie received their diagnosis of diabetes, they began to create artwork with death themes. Although Jamie did not specifically relate this to their new diagnosis, the correlation in timing was striking. Jamie began creating images of graves based on "Minecraft," and began to state that they were a vampire and that I needed to hide from them. Jamie provided detailed instructions for how to engage in the vampire play, which included when to hide and specific music to be played. I continued to provide education about what it meant to be diabetic at the end of the session, and after several sessions of death-themed drawings, vampire play, and diabetes education, Jamie slowly shifted away from the death/vampire themes and reported they felt better and okay with being diabetic.

Goal

Jamie will experience a reduction in their anxiety, as evidenced by structured evaluation, parent/classroom/clinician observation, and self-report.

Objective

Jamie will explore their anxiety through role-play and coping skills practice, as evidenced in the documentation.

Intervention:

- The clinician will encourage self-directed play/art making; the clinician will play with Jamie and make suggestions for coping tools in the context of play scenarios, following Jamie's lead.

Sample note

Jamie continued to express anxiety about their diabetes diagnosis to their mother, but stated they did not want to talk about it in session. The clinician continued to encourage child-centered play and provided psychoeducation about diabetes. Jamie engaged the clinician in vampire-themed play, asking the clinician to run and hide from Jamie, the vampire. Jamie also drew graves for their

"Minecraft" characters, and stated that they had been bitten by the vampire. The clinician asked Jamie about these images, and Jamie stated that it was just part of the game. Jamie acknowledged understanding of the information provided about diabetes, and the clinician validated Jamie's feelings regarding the diagnosis. Jamie denied any suicidal intent or ideation.

STEVIE, CONTINUED

Stevie continued to work on storm-related anxiety throughout our therapeutic relationship. They also reported that they were being bullied at school and that this bothered them; however, beyond this Stevie declined to talk about being bullied. Stevie and I had centered many sessions on learning about tornadoes and related statistics, although Stevie and their mother also occasionally continued to mention bullying and its effects on Stevie. I continued to express to Stevie that the art therapy room was a safe place to explore feelings about bullying and to strategize how to handle bullies in the future, although Stevie continually declined to address the bullying directly. After one such bullying incident Stevie's mother reported that she saw more depressive symptoms and heightened anxiety at home. I encouraged Stevie to express their feelings about the bullying in their artwork and Stevie agreed.

Goal

Stevie stated a desire to apply adaptive coping skills and reduce their anxiety response; progress will be evidenced by assessment, self-report, and session documentation.

Objective

Stevie will identify and practice coping skills to utilize when experiencing anxiety.

Interventions:

- The clinician will encourage Stevie to create imagery/artwork and share about anxiety, as evidenced in the documentation.
- The clinician will provide psychoeducation about coping skills and engage Stevie in identifying and practicing coping skills they would like to try, as evidenced in the documentation.

Sample note

On this day, Stevie's mother reported that Stevie had been upset about being bullied at school. When the clinician asked, Stevie concurred. Stevie stated that they did not want to talk about the bullying. The clinician encouraged Stevie to express how they felt about the bullying through art making, and Stevie agreed. Stevie created a sculpture of a tornado out of Model Magic, and then scattered pieces of Model Magic around it. They then acted out the post-tornado cleanup with the words "FEMA or Red Cross" written on a sheet of paper that they affixed to their shirt. After cleanup, Stevie stated that the bullying had made them feel upset and that they wanted to destroy something. Stevie stated that they felt better after acting out the tornado and cleanup. When the clinician asked who their "FEMA" (Federal Emergency Management Administration) or "Red Cross" could be, they stated their mother and a trusted teacher, and reported they would tell them the next time they were bullied.

PEYTON, CONTINUED

As therapy progressed with Peyton, they shared more about their trauma history. This often occurred in role-plays with LEGO® based on video games known for having gratuitous violence. Peyton engaged in creative play, with LEGO® sets, involving a suicidal criminal. After multiple sessions with similar play themes, Peyton disclosed personal suicidal feelings and contracted for safety (that is, they identified ways to use coping skills and supports rather than harming themself), as well as identified how they felt their family could help. Peyton also identified the "criminals" as their father and at times themself. In a follow-up session, Peyton re-enacted play with similar themes but with more positive outcomes, and stated that they were no longer feeling suicidal. In this session, Peyton highlighted the love and security they felt with their adoptive mother through the character of the criminal's mother who gave the criminal unconditional love, bringing the criminal food from Peyton's favorite restaurant to the jail rather than our previous ending of suicide by cop (that is, placing themselves in a situation where they would be shot by the police as a method of suicide).

Goal

Peyton will be able to engage in healthy expression of emotions related to traumatic experiences and to regulate distressing emotions, as evidenced by therapist observation, self/parent report, and structured evaluation of trauma symptoms.

Objective

The clinician will use a trauma-informed approach to assist Peyton, and will explore and correct inaccurate or unhelpful thoughts and beliefs related to the traumatic memories.

Interventions:

- The clinician will encourage child-centered art and play related to traumatic experiences using Peyton's preferred popular media and art media.
- The clinician will provide psychoeducation regarding coping tools and triggers; Peyton will identify their preferred tools and personal triggers.

Goal

Peyton will experience a reduction in depressive symptoms including irritability, sadness, and suicidal ideation, as assessed through structured assessment.

Objective

Peyton and their family will develop a safety plan.

Interventions:

- The clinician will provide psychoeducation regarding coping tools and triggers; Peyton will identify their preferred tools and personal triggers.
- The clinician and Peyton will meet with their parents to identify and implement a safety plan for home and school.

Objective

The clinician will use a trauma-informed approach to assist Peyton, and will explore and correct inaccurate or unhelpful thoughts and beliefs related to depressive and suicidal feelings.

Interventions:

- The clinician will encourage child-centered art and play related to traumatic experiences using Peyton's preferred popular media and art media.
- The clinician will provide psychoeducation regarding coping tools and triggers; Peyton will identify their preferred tools and personal triggers.

Sample note

Peyton engaged in creative play with LEGO® sets, involving a suicidal criminal. The clinician asked questions about the criminal and their desire to die. The clinician also asked about where the criminal lived, and Peyton provided their address and gave other details that matched their own. Despite the similarities in personal details, Peyton denied that they were the criminal. At Peyton's request, the clinician played the parts of the police and Peyton's family coming to help. In these roles, the clinician provided validation and education about coping skills. Peyton denied having suicidal feelings in this session and stated that they felt they could keep themself safe at home. The clinician informed the parents of Peyton's suicidal statements and their denial of suicidal feelings, and advised that the parents supervise Peyton for suicidal behaviors.

JAYLIN, CONTINUED

Jaylin shared about an abusive relationship they had experienced. They continued to utilize anime-type imagery as they opened up about this situation, and stated that the anime characters represented themselves and their feelings about the relationship. Jaylin reported that anime was a soother, and that engaging in their own anime and manga creation helped them to work through situations and decrease their anxiety.

Goal

Jaylin will develop an awareness of angry thoughts, feelings, and actions, and identify their triggers and alternatives to aggressive anger, as evidenced by session documentation.

Objective

Identify situations, thoughts, or feelings that trigger anger, angry verbal and/or behavioral actions, and the targets of those actions.

Interventions:

- The clinician will develop a level of trust with Jaylin; provide support and empathy to encourage Jaylin to feel safe in expressing their angry emotions through exploration of their feelings in the context of their popular culture interest.

- The clinician will encourage Jaylin to create imagery based on their special interests that explores anger triggers and coping skills.

Goal

Jaylin will work toward resolving the issues surrounding the abusive relationship, resulting in an ability to establish and maintain close interpersonal relationships.

Objective

Build Jaylin's self-esteem and a sense of empowerment, as manifested by an increased number of positive self-descriptive statements and greater participation in extracurricular activities.

Interventions:

- The clinician will encourage Jaylin to create a drawing or sculpture that reflects how the abusive relationship impacted their life and feelings about themself.
- The clinician will encourage Jaylin to create a graphic novel in which they are the hero of the story based on their personal experiences.

Sample note

Jaylin shared a picture they had drawn of themselves (in anime style) regarding how they were feeling. The image was of a young person with a beaten and battered face. Jaylin explained that an ex had continued to harass their family, which caused a lot of stress. They accepted the clinician's suggestion that they create a comic strip about the situation using the third hand (Kramer 2000)—Jaylin directed the clinician in how to create the comic strip on the clinician's computer (due to telehealth constraints in sharing use of the program Storyboard That™). They directed the clinician in what to include in the images. They created a strip showing themself being yelled at by an ex and then two following images where they stood up for themself and felt calm. They guided one additional image where they were crying and their mother was asking what was wrong; they stated that their ex had upset them. They stated that sometimes it was hard to stay away from the ex, even though the ex was mean and upset them. The clinician validated these feelings. Jaylin stated it was helpful to "get these things out," and also identified that their primary coping skills were drawing and watching anime. The clinician provided some education about self-care. The clinician asked Jaylin to make a comic about a time they were angry before the next session in two weeks.

TREATMENT APPLICATIONS/ACTIVITIES

- Encourage the participant to create role-plays based on their interests and goals. The participant directs how the role-play occurs, such as visual art, verbal role-play, video game-based (such as voicing characters):
  - With informed consent role-play may be recorded for future use in session or creation of a video-based art piece (discuss the pros and cons of sharing such things with others, on social media if needed).
- Ask the participant to create a board game or an idea for a video game:
  - Provide the participant with a list of areas that are being addressed in therapy and assist them as desired in creating rules for the game and how such subjects will be addressed (for instance creating a social interaction board game using preferred characters).
  - Play the completed game.

Note: it can be helpful for the participant to play the game with family members to assist in their understanding of the participant's therapeutic goals and desires.

- You may also provide discarded board games or games with missing pieces as art materials for creating a game.
- Alternatively, you may use tools for basic game programming—a quick Google search will provide you with an array of free game programming tools (be sure to try them out on your own first, though, so you can help).
- Create in "Minecraft" creative mode or on Roblox (again, familiarize yourself first so you can troubleshoot, or if the participant is already familiar, ask them to teach you how to use the tools, as this can be a great rapport builder).

• Encourage the participant to create a comic/graphic novel/manga in which they are the hero/anti-hero:
  - Spend some time on the concepts of hero and anti-hero, and encourage storyboarding ideas ahead of creating the comic/graphic novel/manga.
  - You and the participant may make the comic/graphic novel/manga together with simple book-making techniques such as stab binding.
  - There are several make your own comic/graphic novel sketchbooks on the market.
  - Use online software such as Storyboard That™.

• Adapt commercially available storytelling games such as Nanofictionary or Rory's Story Cubes:
  - With Nanofictionary, select targeted cards for the participant to choose from related to the therapeutic focus, and then ask the participant to tell or create a story.

  - With Rory's Story Cubes add to the existing rules: "Create a story featuring your favorite character or place by rolling the dice;" "Draw a storyboard detailing your story" (you may also use a program such as Storyboard That™).

- Construct LEGO® sets themed with preferred topics:
  - Encourage storytelling/acting out what is happening to the characters while building occurs.
  - Further encourage creation of a comic or storyboard-related build and its story.

CHAPTER 11

Popular Culture as Anxiety Mediator

As defined in Chapter 6, participating in popular culture or other special interests can reduce and help to resolve anxiety. Special interests may be used as coping and distress tolerance skills while processing or as preparation for processing anxiety. I observed children creating art and play scenarios around favorite characters experiencing situations similar to those they were anxious about as a means of confronting the anxiety; this overlaps with the previous categories of social facilitation and personal metaphor. I also observed a tendency to gravitate to preferred subjects after disclosing anxiety. The following examples will further illustrate these concepts.

CASE EXAMPLES, TREATMENT PLANNING AND DOCUMENTATION

STEVIE, CONTINUED

In addition to a phobia of thunderstorms and tornadoes, Stevie had social anxiety—not wanting to go anywhere without their parents, not wanting to speak to others. In session we focused on how Stevie could use their interests to feel more comfortable in social settings and as soothers/distress tolerance skills. As Stevie progressed through high school, they became more outgoing and did so through sharing of their interests such as cars and tornadoes. Stevie entered a speech contest, electing to do an educational speech on tornadoes and early warning systems, as their interests shifted from cars to the Weather Channel (as well as Greek and Roman mythology). They made friends on the speech team and shared that they felt less anxious about interacting with their peers, and began talking about having friends more than storms and cars. These appeared to be genuine, supportive friendships and not the ones they had previously dominated with insistence that their peers do only what they wanted or by being bullied by other kids who didn't understand them.

Despite increased interest in storms and knowledge about tornadoes, Stevie continued to have a phobia of tornadoes, which contributed to their difficulty leaving the house at times, in addition to their previously mentioned social anxiety. I asked Stevie to try to use their interest in mythology to help with coping with their storm phobia, and Stevie agreed to do so.

Goal

Stevie stated a desire to apply adaptive coping skills and reduce their anxiety response; progress will be evidenced by assessment, self-report, and session documentation.

Objective

Stevie will identify and practice coping skills to utilize when experiencing anxiety.

Interventions:

- The clinician will encourage Stevie to create imagery/artwork and share about their anxiety, as evidenced in the documentation.
- The clinician and Stevie will research storms and statistics about lethality as well as safety, per Stevie's request.

- The clinician will provide psychoeducation about coping skills and engage Stevie in identifying and practicing coping skills they would like to try, as evidenced in the documentation.
- Stevie will receive a reward for participation in session that Stevie has selected at the beginning of the session, as evidenced in the documentation.

Sample note, session A

Stevie entered the clinician's office and immediately shared about their success on the speech team and the new friends they had met in the speech club. Stevie stated that sharing about their interests in the speech club made it easier to make friends. Stevie reported a desire to invite friends from the speech team to go roller skating, but stated that they were unsure how to do so. The clinician encouraged Stevie to share about what others in the group were interested in, and to identify who they had things in common with and who they might be able to spend time with outside of the club. Stevie identified other students who had given speeches of interest to them, and who had also told Stevie they had done well and shown an interest in tornadoes. Stevie worked with the clinician on a comic strip to practice asking the others to go skating.

Sample note, session B

Stevie reported anxiety over existing storm warnings this day. They stated that they continued to learn about storms as part of giving speeches, and that they wanted to continue working on their storm coping kit that had been started early on in the therapeutic relationship. The clinician accepted this suggestion and encouraged Stevie to come up with decorations to add to the outside of the kit based on their interests, that would help them with distress tolerance during tornado and thunderstorm warnings. Stevie identified another interest, Greek mythology, that they could use as a coping skill, and reported that they planned to tell themself that storms were "Zeus throwing lightning at Hades." Stevie also accepted the clinician's suggestion that the thunder could be noise from Zeus stomping whenever he missed. Stevie decorated their storm coping kit with drawings of Zeus and Hades. They reported feeling better about the storm warning that had been issued that day at the end of the session.

ALEX, CONTINUED

As noted in previous chapters, Alex did not talk much about feelings, and was more willing to share them when able to use metaphors in art making. Alex had become quite attached to an intern who typically worked with us in session. In one session, when the intern was absent, I offered a variety of art supplies including a plain doll to decorate, as Alex had stated a desire to work on such material. Alex chose to work with the doll and began to cut at it with scissors and to dismantle it, pulling out stuffing and allowing bits of armature to poke through the fabric. On completion of work with the doll, Alex stated that they were upset that the intern wasn't there, but that they felt better after the controlled deconstruction of the doll.

Goal

Alex will identify feelings and their triggers and practice coping skills when faced with said triggers, as evidenced by structured evaluation, parent/classroom/clinician observation, and self-report.

Objective

Alex will explore feelings of anger through art making, role-play, and coping skills practice, as evidenced in the documentation.

Intervention:

- The clinician will provide directed art activities when needed, and encourage self-directed art and play to explore feelings of anger and coping skills through use of preferred characters/shows.

Objective

Alex will identify and practice three adaptive coping skills, as evidenced by session notes.

Intervention:

- The clinician will provide psychoeducation regarding coping tools and assist Alex in selecting coping tools that Alex prefers.

Sample note

This day when Alex arrived at the clinician's office, they were quieter than typical, as evidenced by not greeting the clinician as usual, and sitting quietly at the table. The clinician offered Alex supplies including marker pens, paper, scissors, glue, yarn, and a blank cloth doll for decorating, which Alex had requested in a previous session. The clinician attempted to engage Alex in conversation, but Alex did not answer the questions the clinician asked related to Alex's day and how they felt this day. Alex selected the doll blank, some marker pens, and scissors. Alex began to cut and rip at the doll. After approximately 20 minutes Alex stated that the doll was an animatronic from a video game. When the clinician asked how the animatronic felt this day, Alex stated that it was angry, like them. The clinician asked why they were angry and they stated it was because the intern was gone. Alex and the clinician then worked together creating the animatronic's favorite things such as pizza and karaoke (microphone/machine) out of paper for the animatronic to use as coping tools. When the clinician asked Alex to identify their coping tools, Alex drew their video game console on paper and their favorite toy, which was also an animatronic. As Alex left the office, they reported that making and helping the doll helped them feel better.

PEYTON, CONTINUED

Peyton had significant attachment trauma and anxiety, as described in previous chapters. During our therapeutic relationship, Peyton had to have their tonsils removed. Peyton stated that they were anxious about the surgery as they were drawing favorite characters having surgery while asking questions about surgery, listening to my explanations of what would happen. This structure of Peyton drawing these "surgery" type pictures and my explaining and answering their questions about surgery continued for two sessions leading up to the surgery.

Goal

Peyton will be able to engage in a healthy expression of emotions related to traumatic experiences and to regulate distressing emotions, as evidenced by therapist observation, self/parent report, and structured evaluation of trauma symptoms.

Objective

The clinician will use a trauma-informed approach to assist Peyton in exploring and correcting inaccurate or unhelpful thoughts and beliefs related to the traumatic memories.

Interventions:

- The clinician will encourage child-centered art and play related to traumatic experiences using Peyton's preferred popular media and art media.
- The clinician will provide psychoeducation regarding coping

tools and triggers; Peyton will identify their preferred tools and personal triggers.

Goal

Peyton will apply adaptive coping skills and reduce their anxiety, as evidenced by assessment, self-report, and session documentation.

Objective

Peyton will identify and practice coping skills to utilize when experiencing anxiety.

Interventions:

- The clinician will encourage Peyton to draw and share about their anxiety, as evidenced in the documentation.
- The clinician will provide psychoeducation about coping skills and engage Peyton in identifying and practicing coping skills they would like to try when anxious, as evidenced in the documentation.
- Peyton will receive a reward for participation in session that Peyton has selected at the beginning of the session, as evidenced in the documentation.

Sample note

Peyton's mother reported that Peyton would be having their tonsils out soon. Peyton expressed feelings of anxiety over dying while having surgery, and began drawing images of their favorite robot-based video game characters being dismantled by other characters in the game. Peyton had an anxious affect, as evidenced by a frown and increased presence of self-stimming, such as rocking in the session. While Peyton drew, the clinician asked if they would like them to explain how the surgery would work, and Peyton asked that the clinician do so. Peyton continued to draw while the clinician provided education and used a puppet, as a stand-in for

Peyton, to demonstrate where the surgery would occur. Peyton asked several questions regarding where the surgery would be (it happened that the outpatient surgery clinic was visible from the clinician's office and the clinician was able to point it out), whether it would hurt, what would happen after, and other similar questions that the clinician answered. Near the end of the session the clinician asked Peyton if there was a toy or other item that would help them feel better if it was with them at the surgery, and Peyton identified that they'd like to take their stuffed dog. Peyton's affect brightened throughout the session, and they were smiling when they left the office; their rocking had decreased in frequency toward the end of the session.

JAMIE, CONTINUED

Jamie and I continued our art and role-plays based on his favorite characters. They became more open to me interjecting questions, like, "What is Thomas afraid of?" or, "Are the other people in the 'Minecraft' universe afraid of the creepers?" Occasionally they would answer questions like, "What are you afraid of?" and "What makes you feel better?" but mostly they only answered them about their preferred characters. Then suddenly Jamie would show a big leap toward or surpass their goals.

As mentioned in previous chapters, Jamie experienced a great deal of anxiety in our initial meeting and regarding their diabetes diagnosis. Therefore, the goals, objectives, interventions, and sample notes are repeated here from earlier chapters as the reason these interventions were successful was because we were basing them on Jamie's interests, and those inherently provided comfort. Countless hours of popular culture-based art and role-play provided space for addressing Jamie's affective needs and, although rarely directly, addressing the underlying causes of their anxiety, rather than just shaping "unwanted" behavior, and rewarding the right response with a reward, as other approaches encourage.

Note: there is repetition in the following goals, although the case notes represent new examples.

Goal

Jamie and the therapist will build therapeutic rapport through exploring Jamie's interests, as evidenced by Jamie's continued engagement in the therapy process, per documentation.

Objective

Jamie will identify what they would like to focus on in therapy independent of what has been identified by the adults.

Interventions:

- The clinician will encourage Jamie to share likes and dislikes through art and play, as evidenced in the documentation.
- The clinician will encourage Jamie to identify things they would like to change in their life through art and play, as evidenced in session documentation.

Goal

Jamie will experience a reduction in their anxiety, as evidenced by structured evaluation, parent/classroom/clinician observation, and self-report.

Objective

Jamie will explore anxiety through role-play and coping skills practice, as evidenced in the documentation.

Intervention:

- The clinician will encourage self-directed play/art making; the clinician will play with Jamie and make suggestions for coping tools in the context of play scenarios, following Jamie's lead.

Goal

Jamie will experience a reduction in feelings of anger, as evidenced by structured evaluation, parent/classroom/clinician observation, and self-report.

Objective

Jamie will explore feelings of anger through role-play and coping skills practice, as evidenced in the documentation.

Intervention:

- The clinician will encourage self-directed play/art making; the clinician will play with Jamie and make suggestions for coping tools in the context of play scenarios, following Jamie's lead.

Sample note, session A

Jamie continued to be disinterested in talking about conflict with their sibling and peers. The clinician continued to build a welcoming/person-centered space by encouraging Jamie to share more favorite YouTube videos. Jamie shared videos featuring their favorite My Little Ponies. In one video the two My Little Ponies were arguing and were able to resolve the argument. The clinician asked Jamie if they ever have arguments like that, and Jamie stated that these occur with their sibling. Jamie stated that their sibling was annoying and followed them around, which sometimes led to Jamie hitting their sibling to get them to leave them alone. Jamie also stated that it wasn't fair that the sibling didn't have diabetes and got to have candy Jamie couldn't have. The clinician encouraged Jamie to draw a picture of how they could handle the situation differently. Jamie drew an image of them asking their parents for help. Jamie declined to discuss the picture.

Sample note, session B

Jamie continued to report difficulty adjusting to their diabetes diagnosis. When the clinician asked if Jamie would like to make art about it, they stated "no." The clinician then alternatively offered Jamie the opportunity to play with the cat figurines he often played with in session. Jamie agreed and began to set up the figurines. As Jamie engaged in creative play, they set up a computer room for Train Cat (the cat Jamie stated was most like them). Jamie said that Train Cat found out he has to stay at the hospital for a week. When I asked how Train Cat was going to help himself feel better, Jamie stated that Train Cat would watch "Minecraft" videos on YouTube. Jamie also asked the clinician to play a character he created called Dr Miss Kitty, and asked that she visit Train Cat. The clinician did so. Train Cat asked Dr Miss Kitty if they were going to be okay, and Dr Miss Kitty provided validation and reassurance that Train Cat (and Jamie) would be okay. Jamie then asked if they could watch "Minecraft" videos with the clinician; the clinician and Jamie did so. At the end of the session, Jamie's affect had brightened and Jamie stated that they felt less scared.

TOMMIE, CONTINUED

As stated earlier, Tommie experienced both autism and selective mutism, and did not engage in traditional verbal conversation. It is my observation that Tommie was only willing to interact with me because I was willing to interact with them through their interest in superheroes. Therefore, just as with Jamie, the goals, objectives, interventions, and sample notes are repeated here from earlier chapters as the reason these interventions were successful was because we were basing them on Tommie's interests, and those inherently provided comfort.

Goal

Tommie will experience a reduction in their anxiety, which will increase their ability to participate in daily activities such as school and peer play, as desired. Progress will be assessed through ongoing assessments, clinician observation, and self-report.

Objective

The clinician and Tommie will develop a working relationship where the participant feels safe to share their thoughts and feelings.

Interventions:

- The clinician will actively build trust with Tommie through introducing preferred activities and co-engaging in said activities, as evidenced in the documentation.
- The clinician will speak with Tommie without expectation of a response, explaining to Tommie the therapeutic process, and inviting Tommie to continue art and play-based engagement, as evidenced in the documentation.

Sample note

Tommie did not interact with the clinician verbally in this session. Tommie went to their room while the clinician spoke to their mother. The mother shared that Tommie continued to have difficulty in school due to lack of verbal interaction. When Tommie returned, they invited the clinician to play with Avengers LEGO® sets, as they had done before. The clinician engaged in person-centered play with Tommie, asking occasional questions regarding school. Tommie did not answer verbally but did act out school-like scenarios with the LEGO® blocks. The clinician will continue using person-centered art and play with Tommie to continue development of rapport and comfort with the clinician.

JAYLIN, REVISITED

Jaylin shared about their concern over a friend who had gone missing. The following is an example related to Jaylin reporting that anime was a soother, and that engaging in their own anime and manga creation helped them to work through situations and decrease their anxiety.

Goal

Jaylin will develop an awareness of angry thoughts, feelings, and actions, and identify their triggers and alternatives to aggressive anger, as evidenced by session documentation.

Objective

Identify situations, thoughts, or feelings that trigger anger, angry verbal and/or behavioral actions, and the targets of those actions.

Interventions:

- The clinician will develop a level of trust with Jaylin; provide support and empathy to encourage Jaylin to feel safe in expressing their angry emotions through exploration of feelings in the context of their popular culture interest.
- The clinician will encourage Jaylin to create imagery based in their special interests that explores anger triggers and coping skills.

Goal

Jaylin will work toward resolving the issues surrounding the abusive relationship, resulting in an ability to establish and maintain close interpersonal relationships.

Objective

Build self-esteem and a sense of empowerment, as manifested by an increased number of positive self-descriptive statements and greater participation in extracurricular activities.

Interventions:

- The clinician will encourage Jaylin to create a drawing or sculpture that reflects how the abusive relationship impacted their life and feelings about themself.
- The clinician will encourage Jaylin to create a graphic novel in which they are the hero of the story, based on their personal experiences.

Sample note

Jaylin shared that they had been taking a new medication for their irritability, and that it had been helping. They shared that they continued to work on their hero story narrative and that they had added rescuing a missing friend. The clinician provided validation of their feelings and encouraged Jaylin to share about how they related to the missing friend. Jaylin shared about a time they had run away when they were younger. Jaylin acknowledged that they had run away out of anger, and worked on and then shared a drawing they created about their anger—which illustrated themself turning into a devil with angel wings. They stated the wings showed they were truly good, but that was hard to see when they were angry. They shared that their fidgets and drawing anime continue to help when they get upset, and that they continued to do better with their anger.

TREATMENT APPLICATIONS/ACTIVITIES

- Foster time for the participants to focus on/create about their preferred interests as a coping skill:

  - Encourage the participant to knead or sculpt dough, draw, or paint preferred interests (without expectation for specific content to be explored). Ask the following questions:

    How do you feel when you create this image?

    What do you notice about how your body reacts? Where in your body do you experience these feelings?

    Are there other things that help you feel this way? (if positive)

    Are there things that help you feel better? (if negative)

    When/how can you use your character/interest and your art to feel better when you are anxious?

  - Facilitate use of LEGO® and other themed art kits based on the participant's interests.

    Note: although such things have often been viewed as not creative or as being stereotypical art, these types of art making often provide comfort based in familiarity of subject matter or set rules to follow.

- Create a cope ahead kit featuring soothers based on expressed interests (this might be a physical box of soothers or perhaps a Google doc with links in it, or a combination of multiple sources), including, for example:

  - If the participant spends time watching YouTube or TikTok videos about making slime, make slime and include this in the kit.

  - If the participant finds music calming, create a playlist including favorite songs; this can be paired with making an "album cover," which can serve as a visual soother.

  - Coloring pages of preferred interests.

- Small, themed LEGO® sets.
- If interests include popular media-based card games or collectors' cards, include cards in the kit. The participant can design their own cards, for example:

  What would you look like as a Pokémon? What would your powers be? How would you defend yourself from anxious feelings?

  If you were a baseball player, what team would you play for? What would your stats be? What coping skills would you use for the big game?
- If this is a physical box, encourage decoration of the outside of the box featuring interests. If accessible, maintain a supply of interest-themed stickers to assist with decoration.
- If art making is a soother, include preferred art supplies.

  Note: the specific size of the kit will depend on what is included and need for portability. The examples for what to include in the box can also be used as independent directives.

- Provide doll blanks or supplies for making own dolls/sock animals or puppets as a transitional object (many participants will naturally gravitate toward making their doll based on their popular culture interests).
- Engage in creative play with themed toys—follow the participant's lead in the direction of play and provide validation and thoughtful questions while doing so:
  - If the participant enjoys making videos, obtain informed consent, and make that part of the process. The participant can then review the video content, and this will provide more opportunity for processing in session. The participant

may choose to make the video into a longer film project, encouraging further exploration of this play and creative review of it as a coping tool.

- Encourage the participant to create a comic/graphic novel/manga in which they are the hero/anti-hero:
  - Spend some time on the concepts of hero and anti-hero, and encourage storyboarding ideas ahead of creating the comic/graphic novel/manga.
  - The clinician and participant may make the comic/graphic novel/manga together with simple book-making techniques such as stab binding.
  - There are several make your own comic/graphic novel sketchbooks on the market.
  - Use online software such as Storyboard That™.
- Ask the participant to create a board game or idea for a video game:
  - Provide the participant with a list of areas that are being addressed in therapy, and assist them as desired in creating rules for the game and how such subjects will be addressed (for instance, creating a social interaction board game using preferred characters).
  - Play the completed game.

    Note: it can be helpful for the participant to play the game with family members to assist in their understanding of the therapeutic goals and desires of the participant.
  - You may also provide discarded board games or games with missing pieces as art materials for creation of the game.
  - Alternatively, you may use tools for basic game pro-

gramming—a quick Google search will provide you with an array of free game programming tools (be sure to try them out on your own first, so you can help).

- Create in "Minecraft" creative mode or on Roblox (again, familiarize yourself first so you can troubleshoot, or if the participant is already familiar, ask them to teach you how to use the tools, as this can be a great rapport builder).

CHAPTER 12

Popular Culture as Communication Clarifier

Finally, I observed that the use of popular culture can indicate a participant's understanding of a concept. Concepts may include feelings or social rules or other things that may be necessary to define or explain. The most salient example for me was when Jamie sculpted a set of characters representing themself, my intern, and myself, based on a favorite video game, and subsequently sent their character to therapy, with the characters representing the intern and myself. Another vivid example included when Alex shared about building models in history class out of LEGO® to help them understand the concepts and places that were talked about. These and other examples are provided in more detail below.

CASE EXAMPLES, TREATMENT PLANNING AND DOCUMENTATION

JAMIE, CONTINUED

Early on in our therapeutic relationship, Jamie created a play scenario reminiscent of a conversation we had about the consequences of anger toward their younger sibling. The conversation had included the purpose of therapy and the potential for hospitalization if Jamie continued to have aggressive outbursts, potentially endangering their sibling. After this conversation Jamie made sculptures of characters based on their favorite video game. When these sculptures were dry, they engaged them in creative play in a small town that they constructed from LEGO®. Jamie sent their character to therapy, where the two other characters served as the therapist and intern. Although Jamie did not directly identify the characters as themself, the therapist, or intern, the character interactions made their representation clear.

Goal

Jamie will experience a reduction in feelings of anger, as evidenced by structured evaluation, parent/classroom/clinician observation, and self-report.

Objective

Jamie will explore feelings of anger through role-play and coping skills practice, as evidenced in the documentation.

Intervention:

- The clinician will encourage self-directed play/art making; the clinician will play with Jamie and make suggestions for coping tools in the context of play scenarios, following Jamie's lead.

Sample note

Jamie reported that they had gotten along better with their sibling this week, and that they had not hit their sibling at all (and their mother concurred). Jamie stated that they didn't want to talk about it anymore than that. The clinician encouraged Jamie to play with characters they had created the previous week, when the clinician provided psychoeducation about aggression and therapy. Jamie first built a LEGO® town for the characters and then destroyed it, taking it apart and tossing the pieces around while holding one character. Jamie then sent this character to therapy with the other two, and asked the intern and the clinician to act as those characters. The clinician and intern used a child-centered approach and followed Jamie's lead and asked "therapy questions," provided "art directives" for Jamie's character, and reiterated some of the psychoeducation from the previous week. Jamie then announced that their character had been successfully treated and would no longer destroy the town.

ALEX, CONTINUED

As Alex continued to build coping and soother skills, they shared about use of LEGO® to build models for history class. Alex stated that being able to build models helped them understand the concepts, retain the information, and demonstrate understanding of the material in ways that traditional educational methods did not. We adapted this to use in therapy sessions where Alex could explain situations and feelings to me through building models, and we could use said models to address Alex's goals.

Goal

Alex will identify feelings and their triggers and practice coping skills when faced with said triggers, as evidenced by structured evaluation, parent/classroom/clinician observation, and self-report.

Objective

Alex will explore feelings of anxiety through art making, role-play, and coping skills practice, as evidenced in the documentation.

Interventions:

- The clinician will provide directed art activities when needed, and encourage self-directed art and play to explore feelings of anxiety and coping skills through use of preferred characters/shows.

- The clinician will encourage Alex to use preferred interests to convey feelings and understanding of concepts.

Objective

Alex will identify and practice three adaptive coping skills, as evidenced by session notes.

Interventions:

- The clinician will provide psychoeducation regarding coping tools and assist Alex in selecting coping tools that Alex prefers.
- The clinician will encourage Alex to use preferred interests to convey feelings and understanding of concepts.

Sample note

Alex reported that they had been feeling depressed. The clinician encouraged Alex to create an image of what depression felt like to them. Alex created a LEGO® build and used a *Star Wars* figure to represent themself. Alex used dark-colored LEGO® to build a small structure, placed themself in it, and put a top on the structure. Alex then moved a lamp so a small amount of light could shine in through the structure's door. Alex stated that they felt alone in the dark, like this figure, but that they could see a light shining. Alex shared they were trying to figure out ways to get to the light, and engaged in conversation with the clinician about what was helping them feel better and what they felt their depression triggers were.

PEYTON, CONTINUED

I find it very important to understand and be at least somewhat knowledgeable about my participants' interests as it helps me to understand them better and to integrate these interests into sessions. Working in this way helps me to continue to adapt rewards (where applicable), and to adapt goals, materials, and art directives. After spending some time focused on the cops and robbers-type video games, Peyton's interests started to evolve, and they began to show interest in war-based video games and *Star Trek*. Peyton also stated they were interested in developing better communication skills. I asked Peyton to explain to me their new interests and goals in these things in a drawing. Peyton agreed to do so and used the drawings to help me understand more about them and from where the interests had been sparked.

Goal

Peyton articulated a desire to improve their communication skills, particularly as related to family and peers. Progress will be measured through self-report and structured assessment of social anxiety symptoms.

Objective

Assess specific areas of communication on which Peyton would like to work.

Interventions:

- The clinician will engage Peyton in communication-style assessments to help identify areas Peyton feels are in need of development.
- The clinician will engage Peyton in the creation of a comic to identify situations where they felt they could improve in communication skills/identify communication goals.

Goal

Peyton will apply adaptive coping skills and reduce anxiety, as evidenced by assessment, self-report, and session documentation.

Objective

Peyton will identify and practice coping skills to utilize when experiencing anxiety.

Interventions:

- The clinician will encourage Peyton to draw and share about anxiety, as evidenced in the documentation.
- The clinician will provide psychoeducation about coping skills and engage Peyton in identifying and practicing coping skills they would like to try when anxious, as evidenced in the documentation.
- Peyton will receive a reward for participation in session that Peyton has selected at the beginning of the session, as evidenced in the documentation.

Sample note

In session, Peyton expressed a desire to improve their communication with family and friends. They stated that they were watching *Star Trek* with their parents and that they wanted to figure out how to apply "the Prime Directive" to interactions with their friends and family, and also when it was okay to violate it. Peyton defined this as, "The Prime Directive prohibits Starfleet personnel and spacecraft from interfering in the normal development of any society, and mandates that any Starfleet vessel or crew member is expendable to prevent violation of this rule" (Okuda, Okuda, & Mirek 1999). The clinician asked them to create an image of "the Prime Directive." Peyton completed an image and stated it was of Captain Kirk and Spock, and that Captain Kirk had cloned Spock so they could fight and end the Afghanistan War. Peyton shared that he thought that this type of interfering was okay, and stated that they had made this image because they'd been watching *Star Trek* with their father who had served in the war. The clinician validated Peyton's feelings and encouraged Peyton to continue making art about "the Prime Directive" until the next session, and to bring it in to discuss further.

CAL, CONTINUED

As mentioned earlier, Cal was fond of the show *The Office*, and we used the show to help Cal identify others' emotions and body language and to practice interactions for which they were nervous or unsure. However, we also utilized *The Office* to help identify ways they had successfully communicated and instances where others had communication challenges. In practicing autism positive art therapy it is important to shift the burden for relationship change to the relationship itself and others in that relationship, rather than put the full burden on the autistic participant.

Goal

"I want to be better able to identify others' feelings from what they say and do." Progress will be evidenced by therapist observation and Cal's self-report and artwork.

Objective

Cal will practice identifying emotions based on facial expression and body language; progress will be tracked through self-report and therapist observation.

Intervention:

- The therapist will provide video clips and structured discussion/practice based on said clips to assist Cal in practicing emotion identification, as documented in session notes.

Objective

Cal will practice understanding of idioms, similes, metaphors, jokes, and sarcasm; progress will be tracked through self-report and therapist observation.

Intervention:

- The therapist will provide video clips and structured discussion/practice based on said clips to assist Cal in identifying and understanding abstract language/when to ask questions regarding abstract language, as documented in session notes.

Objective

Cal will engage in social practice to encourage generalization of skills learned related to emotion identification/understanding other social communication.

Intervention:

- Cal will practice social scenarios through creating a graphic novel featuring preferred characters.

Sample note

Cal continued to report conflict with their mother. Cal stated that they had a difficult time identifying the signs that their mother was becoming frustrated with them. Cal and the clinician continued to watch episodes of *The Office* to help identify/understand body language and other forms of communication. The clinician encouraged Cal to identify which character they were most like and which their mother resembled. The clinician engaged Cal in cognitive restructuring to identify areas where Cal had successfully communicated and their mother had not. Cal created a comic strip illustrating these examples to assist in an upcoming family therapy session. Cal engaged actively in the psychoeducational activity and practice as well as in the cognitive restructuring and family therapy planning.

TREATMENT APPLICATIONS/ACTIVITIES

- From early in the therapeutic relationship, encourage introductory artwork, introducing themselves and their preferences. Co-participate in this—participants often want to know more about us, and willingness to share small things goes a long way:
  - Mutually share clips from preferred shows, movies, and videos.
  - Play video games together in initial sessions as part of a rapport-building process.
  - Provide coloring sheets, LEGO® sets, and other themed materials from preferred topics.
- As the therapist, do some research on your own about the participant's preferred topics so you can use them in session to help clarify concepts:
  - For instance, learn about Michael Scott from *The Office* to talk about socially awkward or non-preferred social behavior.
- Ask the participant to explain what makes them interested in their preferred interests. This will help you to use these to clarify other concepts in therapy.
- Ask the participant if what they discuss in therapy reminds them of preferred interests. Encourage creation of imagery based on this.
- Encourage the participant to create a comic/graphic novel/manga in which they are the hero/anti-hero as a way to help explain what they want to address/how they feel about certain situations, etc.:
  - Spend some time on the concepts of hero and anti-hero,

and encourage storyboarding ideas ahead of creating the comic/graphic novel/manga.

 - You and the participant may make the comic/graphic novel/manga together with simple book-making techniques such as stab binding.
 - There are several make your own comic/graphic novel sketchbooks on the market.
 - Use online software such as Storyboard That™.

- Watch clips of movies, TV, YouTube videos, etc. in session to assist in illustrating concepts, or encourage participants to request clips to explain situations when they feel it would be helpful.

CHAPTER 13

Final Thoughts and Resources

Encouraging an art therapy participant's inclusion of special interests in the art therapy setting is one way that art therapists can be autism and neurodiversity positive. As Henley (1989, 2018) indicated, when participants share their special interests with a therapist, they are giving the therapist a window into their psyches. It is through these interests that the therapist and participant can build relationships and address needs. It may be the impulse of therapists to quiet these obsessions in the therapy setting, but those who do risk losing valuable information and doing a disservice to the participant. This book provides a facilitative framework for and specific examples of how popular culture special interests can assist in the development of the therapeutic relationship. These interests provide opportunities for the therapist to enter the participant's world, to model and practice joint attention, and to assist in developing these interests into coping skills. In special interest-based interactions, clinicians partner with participants in their development of personal metaphors based on these interests.

Practicing with a neurodiversity and autism positive approach challenges the art therapist in several important ways. Recognition of neurodiversity demands a strength-based approach that includes respect for participant autonomy, and acknowledgement that neurodivergent ways of thinking can be an asset. The ability to hyper-focus on perseverative interests for hours, days, or years represents an adaptive skill that may serve the participant in other areas. Special interests provide opportunities for comfort, self-expression, communication and connection, and personal growth. I believe that art therapists' ability to acknowledge and integrate participants' special interests may be key in developing the therapeutic relationship and building successful art therapy interventions.

Henley (1989) observed more than 30 years prior to the publishing of this book that paying attention to the special interests of participants with autism was the key to truly understanding them. I came to the same conclusion before ever reading the words from Henley, and I suspect that many other art therapists have as well. Writing this book and completing the dissertation it is based on afforded me the opportunity to flesh out how engagement of these interests can enhance art therapy practice and deepen the therapeutic relationship through encouraging participants to share and explore their popular culture special interests in session. Encouraging participant engagement of these interests is autism positive in that it acknowledges and respects their neurodivergence by not expecting them to fit the neurotypical models of traditional therapy, which equate popular culture with stereotype and surface-level interactions. The special interest communication theory (SICT) facilitative framework acknowledges that popular culture imagery and metaphor can be deeply and personally meaningful. I hope you find this book and the examples within useful in your practice of autism and neurodiversity positive art therapy.

The following are useful resources for integration of special interests in art therapy. These things are forever evolving, however, and so there are likely several useful resources that I have not included.

NEURODIVERSITY OR AUTISM POSITIVE RESOURCES

Autism Self Advocacy Network (ASAN): https://autisticadvocacy.org

Autistic Women & Nonbinary Network (AWN): https://awnnetwork.org

Cooper, K., Smith, L. G. E., & Russell, A. (2017). Social identity, self-esteem, and mental health in autism. *European Journal of Social Psychology 47*(7), 844–854. https://doi.org/10.1002/ejsp.2297

Neurodiversity Hub: www.neurodiversityhub.org

Therapist Neurodiversity Collective: https://therapistndc.org

RELATED POP-CULTURE AND THERAPY RESOURCES

Geek Therapy: https://geektherapy.org

Geek Therapeutics: www.geektherapeutics.com

Rubin, L. C. (2011). *Popular culture in counseling, psychotherapy and play-based interventions*. Springer.

Superhero Therapy: www.superhero-therapy.com

HELPFUL ART THERAPY READINGS

Austin, B. D. (2009). Renewing the debate: Digital technology in art therapy and the creative process. *Art Therapy: Journal of the American Art Therapy Association 26*(2), 83–85. https://doi.org/10.1080/07421656.2009.10129745

Bragge, A., & Fenner, P. (2009). The emergence of the "Interactive Square" as an approach to art therapy with children on the autistic spectrum. *International Journal of Art Therapy 14*(1), 17–28. https://doi.org/10.1080/17454830903006323

Brown, C., & Garner, R. L. (2017). Serious gaming, virtual, and immersive environments in art therapy. In R. L. Garner (ed.), *Digital art therapy: Materials, methods, and applications* (pp.192–205). Jessica Kingsley Publishers.

Carlton, N. R. (2014). Digital culture and art therapy. *The Arts in Psychotherapy 41*, 41–45. https://doi.org/10.1016/j.aip.2013.11.006

Dunn-Snow, P. (1993). What's so special about Teenage Mutant Ninja Turtles? *American Journal of Art Therapy 31*(4), 102.

Potash, J. S. (2009). Fast food art, talk show therapy: The impact of mass media on adolescent art therapy. *Art Therapy 26*(2), 52–57. https://doi.org.10.1080/07421656.2009.10129746

Stallings, J. W. (2021). Special Interest Connection Framework: Integrating Pop Culture Into Art Therapy With Autistic Individuals. *Art Therapy: Journal of the American Art Therapy Association*. https://doi.org.10.1080/07421656.2021.2013718

Thong, S. A. (2007). Redefining the tools of art therapy. *Art Therapy: Journal of the American Art Therapy Association 24*(2), 52–58. https://doi.org.10.1080/07421656.2009.10129746

Van Lith, T., Stallings, J. W., & Harris, C. E. (2017). Discovering good practice for art therapy with children who have Autism Spectrum Disorder: The results of a small scale survey. *The Arts in Psychotherapy 54*, 78–84. https://doi.org/10.1016/j.aip.2017.01.002

Williams, R. R. (Prod. & Dir.) (2016) Life Animated: A Story of Sidekicks, Heroes and Autism [Motion picture]. A&E Indie Films.

HELPFUL DIGITAL ART PROGRAMS

Digital art programs are helpful as you can often upload images of characters into them for manipulation, and many participants enjoy digital art making. This is a quickly changing area, however, and these may not be an accurate representation of what is available to you as you read this book.

Blender (digital 3D/2D/animation): www.blender.org

Brushes XP (Apple only) (drawing app with drawing capture to make videos of your process): https://apps.apple.com/gb/app/brushes-xp/id866047421

FlipaClip™ (app for making digital flip books/animations): https://flipaclip.us

ibisPaint (drawing app with drawing capture to make videos of your process): https://ibispaint.com

Sculptris for Windows (digital 3D modeling/sculpting): https://sculptris.en.softonic.com

Shadow's Edge (therapeutic art journaling game app): www.shadowsedge.com

Storyboard That™ (storyboarding online program): www.storyboardthat.com

It is also helpful to have access to:

- Popular social media apps (in order to see viral videos that participants often enjoy and that may influence their interests).
- A laptop and/or a table on which app-based games can be played (you can ask that the participant bring their own if needed).
- Streaming services.
- A gaming system.

Make a note of any additional useful related resources on the following blank page.

CONSIDERATIONS FOR POPULAR CULTURE WITH YOUR CLIENTS

This table can be obtained as an infographic on the author's website: www.arttherapyandneurodiversity.com

What are your client's preferences?	Does your client want to include it?
Pop-culture-based interests take many forms and some are easier than others to integrate into the therapeutic process. Examples include but are not limited to: • sports • video games • TV • movies • YouTube • books • comics • music • politics • religion • popular toys • superheroes.	They spend a significant amount of time talking about or participating in these special interests – one might call these obsessions or preservations. They are more willing to communicate when special interests are a part of the conversation. The special interests do not cause distress or cause distress that can be or needs to be addressed in therapy. They specifically request its inclusion.

cont.

Is it appropriate to explore pop culture in your setting? Restrictions such as company policy, internet filters, and auditing procedures may lead to challenges in employing popular culture in some settings. These may prohibit watching YouTube, playing video games, or other forms of pop culture from being integrated in session. If such restrictions apply consider sticking with encouraging traditional art making based on these interests. Themed coloring pages and collage materials can help facilitate integration.	**Can these interests further treatment goals?** Case example for goal of anxiety reduction: Jamie liked Thomas the Tank Engine, like many individuals with ASD. When he was anxious about something, like the start of the school year, something disastrous would happen to Thomas. Jamie would role-play or draw Thomas and the village of Sodor experiencing a terrible tornado. I encouraged Jamie to problem solve to help Thomas, which often led to helping Jamie too.
Functions of pop culture in neurodiverse art therapy • behavioral reward • social initiator (rapport builder) • social facilitator (encourage engagement in non-preferred topics) • personal metaphor • anxiety mediator • communication clarifier (communicate meaning or understanding).	**Cautions** Too much time using technology-based interests can lead to: • sleep disruption • overstimulation • increased social difficultires • increased anxiety • shortened attention span • addiction to screen-based technology. See: www.psychologytoday.com/us/blog/mental-wealth/201612/autism-and-screen-time-special-brains-special-risks Note: adapting these interests to art and play-based activities can help in addressing these concerns.

EMPLOYING POPULAR CULTURE IN NEURODIVERSE ART THERAPY INTERACTIONS

The following information can be obtained as an infographic at www.arttherapyandneurodiversity.com

Pop culture as a behavioural reward

To reward desired behaviours.
Offering pop-culture-based rewards (stickers, watching YouTube, playing video games) upon completion of one or more desired behaviours.

Pop culture as social initiator

To initiate social relationships through sharing interests.
Participating in video games, watching YouTube together, joint attention through making art about popular culture interests.

Pop culture as social facilitator

To serve as social buffer for uncomfortable/undesirable topics.
Encouraging and co-creating artwork, comic strips, or role-play featuring preferred characters and topics to explore non-preferred topics, and to identify and process relevant concepts, for instance emotions of coping skills.

Pop culture as personal metaphor

To resolve conflict through pop-culture-based role-play or artwork.
Encouraging creation of personal metaphors based in pop-culture special interests, such as addressing sibling conflict through artwork about conflict within a video game.

Pop culture as anxiety mediator

To interact via pop culture during or prior to processing anxiety, directly or indirectly.

Using special interests as a primer for addressing root anxiety, such as creating video-game-themed art prior to addressing anxiety. Or developing special interests into coping skills.

Pop culture as communication clarifier

To indicate or encourage understanding through pop-culture references and examples.

Using special interest examples to clarify concepts, by the therapist or client, for instance using character interactions from a TV show to explain the dynamics of the relationship.

References

Anderson, M., & Jiang, J. (2018). Teens, social media & technology 2018. www.pewinternet.org/2018/05/31/teens-social-media-technology-2018

APA (American Psychiatric Association) (2013). *Diagnostic and statistical manual of mental disorders* (5th ed.). Author.

ASAN (Autistic Self Advocacy Network) (2015, July 28). ASAN praises ED letter urging schools to look beyond ABA. https://autisticadvocacy.org/2015/07/asan-praises-ed-letter-urging-schools-to-look-beyond-aba

ASAN (Autistic Self Advocacy Network) (2017). About. https://autisticadvocacy.org/about-asan

ASAN (Autistic Self Advocacy Network) (2019). Positions Statements. https://autisticadvocacy.org/about-asan/position-statements

Attwood, T. (1998). *Asperger's syndrome: A guide for parents and professionals.* Jessica Kingsley Publishers.

Attwood, T. (2004). Cognitive behavior therapy for children and adults with Asperger's syndrome. *Behaviour Change 21*, 147–161. https://doi.org/10.1375/bech.21.3.147.55995

Austin, B. D. (2009). Renewing the debate: Digital technology in art therapy and the creative process. *Art Therapy: Journal of the American Art Therapy Association 26*(2), 83–85. https://doi.org/10.1080/07421656.2009.10129745

Baker, J. (2006). *The social skills picture book for high school and beyond.* Future Horizons.

Bauminger, N. (2002). The facilitation of social-emotional understanding and social interaction in high-functioning children with autism: Intervention outcomes. *Journal of Autism and Developmental Disorders 32*(4), 283–298. https://doi.org/10.1023/A:1016378718278

Beck, J. S. (2011). *Cognitive behavior therapy: Basics and beyond* (2nd ed.). Guilford Press.

"Bendy and the Ink Machine" [Computer software] (2008). Complete edition. https://joeydrewstudios.com/batim

Benjamin, J. (1988). *The bonds of love: Psychoanalysis, feminism, and the problem of domination*. Pantheon Books.

Bergman, A. (2000). Preface. In M. Mahler, A. Pine, & A. Bergman, *The psychological birth of the human infant*. Basic Books.

Bettelheim, B. (1967). *The empty fortress: Infantile autism and the birth of the self*. Free Press of Glencoe.

Betts, D., Harmer, R., & Schumelevich, G. (2014). The contributions of art therapy in treatment, assessment, and research with people who have autism spectrum disorders. In V. W. Hu (ed.), *Frontiers in autism research: New horizons for diagnosis and treatment* (pp.627–655). World Scientific.

Blazhenkova, O., & Kozhevnikov, M. (2009). The new object-spatial-verbal cognitive style model: Theory and measurement. *Applied Cognitive Psychology 23*, 638–663.

Bowlby, J. (1958). The nature of the child's tie to his mother. *International Journal of Psychoanalysis 39*, 350–373.

Boyd, B. A., Conroy, M. A., Richmond Mancil, G., Nakao, T., & Alter, P. J. (2007). Effects of circumscribed interests on the social behavior of children with autism spectrum disorders. *Journal of Autism and Developmental Disorders 37*, 1550–1561. https://doi.org/10.1007/s10803-006-0286-8

Boyd, B. A., McBee, M., Holtzclaw, T., Baranek, G. T., & Bodfish, J. W. (2009). Relationships among repetitive behaviors, sensory features, and executive functions in high functioning autism. *Research in Autism Spectrum Disorders 3*, 959–966. https://doi.org/10.1016/j.rasd.2009.05.003

Bragge, A., & Fenner, P. (2009). The emergence of the 'Interactive Square' as an approach to art therapy with children on the autistic spectrum. *International Journal of Art Therapy 14*(1), 17–28. https://doi.org/10.1080/17454830903006323

Brown, C., & Garner, R. L. (2017). Serious gaming, virtual, and immersive environments in art therapy. In R. L. Garner (ed.), *Digital art therapy: Materials, methods, and applications* (pp.192–205). Jessica Kingsley Publishers.

Burt, S. (2017). The promise and potential of fan fiction. *The New Yorker*, August 23. www.newyorker.com/books/page-turner/the-promise-and-potential-of-fan-fiction

Camargo, S. P. H., Rispoli, M., Ganz, J., Hong, E. R., Davis, H., & Mason, R. (2016). Behaviorally based intervention for teaching social interaction skills to children with ASD in inclusive settings: A meta-analysis. *Journal of Behavioral Education 25*, 223–248. https://doi.org/10.1007/s10864-015-9240-1

Cassidy, S. A., Gould, K., Townsend, E., Pelton, M., Robertson, A. E., & Rodgers, J. (2020). Is camouflaging autistic traits associated with suicidal thoughts and behaviours? Expanding the interpersonal psychological theory of suicide in an undergraduate student sample. *Journal of Autism and Developmental Disorders* 50(10), 3638–3648. https://doi.org/10.1007/s10803-019-04323-3

Carlton, N. (2014). Digital culture and art therapy. *The Arts in Psychotherapy 41*, 41–45. https://doi.org/10.1016/j.aip.2013.11.006

Charlton, J. (1998). *Nothing about us without us: Disability oppression and empowerment*. University of California Press.

Cooper, K., Smith, L. G., & Russell, A. (2017). Social identity, self-esteem, and mental health in autism. *European Journal of Social Psychology 47*(7), 844–854.

Creed, T. (2015). An introduction to CBT for people with autism spectrum disorder [Blog post]. https://beckinstitute.org/blog/an-introduction-to-cbt-for-people-with-an-autism-spectrum-disorder

Crooke, P., & Winner, M. G. (2021). Respecting neurodiversity by helping social learners meet their personal goals. [Blog post] *25 Yrs! Social Thinking*, February 12. www.socialthinking.com/Articles?name=respecting-neurodiversity-help-social-learners-meet-goals

Cutler, E. (2004). *A thorn in my pocket*. Future Horizons.

David, D., Cristea, I., & Hofmann, S. G. (2018). Why cognitive behavioral therapy is the current gold standard of psychotherapy. *Frontiers in Psychology 9*(4). https://doi.org/10.3389/fpsyt.2018.00004

Dolphin, M., Byers, A., Goldsmith, A., & Jones, R.E. (2014). *Psychodynamic art therapy practice with people on the autistic spectrum*. Routledge

Dunckley, V. L. (2015). *Reset your child's brain: A four week plan to end meltdowns, raise grades and boost social skills by reversing the effects of electronic screen time*. New World Library.

Dunn-Snow, P. (1993). What's so special about Teenage Mutant Ninja Turtles? *American Journal of Art Therapy 31*(4), 102.

Durrani, H. (2014). Facilitating attachment in children with autism through art therapy: A case study. *Journal of Psychotherapy Integration 24*(2), 99–108. https://doi.org/10.1037/a0036974

Durrani, H. (2019). Art therapy's scope to address impaired attachment in children with ASD and comorbid SID. *Art Therapy 37*(3), 131–138. https://doi.org/10.1080/07421656.2019.1677063

Durrani, H. (2021). Sensory-based relational art therapy approach (S-BRATA): A framework for art therapy with children with ASD. *Art Therapy 38*(2), 78–86. https://doi.org/10.1080/07421656.2020.1718054

Edwards, D. (2014). *Art therapy* (2nd edn). SAGE Publications Ltd.

Elkis-Abuhoff, D. (2008). Art therapy applied to an adolescent with Asperger's syndrome. *Arts in Psychotherapy 35*(4), 262–270. https://doi.org/10.1016/j.aip.2008.06.007

Elkis-Abuhoff, D. (2009). Art therapy and adolescents with Asperger's syndrome. In S. L. Brooke (ed.), *The use of creative therapies with autism spectrum disorders* (pp.19–41). Charles C. Thomas.

Evans, K., & Dubowski, J. (2001). *Art therapy with children on the autistic spectrum*. Jessica Kingsley Publishers.

Gerity, L. A. (2001). Josie, Winnicott, and the hungry ghosts. *Art Therapy: Journal of the American Art Therapy Association 18*(1), 44–49. https://doi.org/10.1080/07421656.2001.10129449

Gillespie, A., & Cornish, A. (2009). Intersubjectivity: Towards a dialogical analysis. *Journal for the Theory of Social Behaviour 40*(1), 19–46. https://doi.org/10.1111/j.1468-5914.2009.00419.x

Grandin, T., & Panek, R. (2013). *The autistic brain: Helping different kinds of minds succeed*. Mariner Books.

Gray, C. (1994). *Comic strip conversations*. Future Horizons.

Guerney, L. (2001). Child-centered play therapy. *International Journal of Play Therapy 10*(2), 13–31. https://doi.org/10.1037/h0089477

Hagopian, L. P., Hardesty, S. L., & Gregory, M. (2015). Applied behavior analysis from the Neurobehavioral Unit (NBU). www.kennedykrieger.org/patient-care/centers-and-programs/neurobehavioral-unit-nbu/applied-behavior-analysis

Hartman, A. (2020). Telling my story in the gallery: Art therapy with females on the autism spectrum. *Art Therapy: Journal of the American Art Therapy Association 37*(4), 208–212.

Henley, D. R. (1989). Nadia revisited: A study into the nature of regression in the autistic savant syndrome. *Art Therapy: Journal of the American Art Therapy Association 6*(2), 43–56. https://doi.org/10.1080/07421656.1989.10758866

Henley, D. R. (2018). *Creative response activities for children on the spectrum: A therapeutic and educational memoir*. Routledge.

Humburg, K. D. (2016). Lights, camera, autism: A movie-based art therapy guidebook [Unpublished Master's project]. Emporia State University.

Humburg, K., & Wolf Bordonaro, G. (2017, November). Lights, camera, autism: Traversing autism through movie-based art therapy. Paper presented at the Annual Conference of the American Art Therapy Association, Albuquerque, NM.

Isserow, J. (2008). Looking together: Joint attention in art therapy. *International Journal of Art Therapy 13*(1), 34–42. https://doi.org/10.1080/17454830802002894

Isserow, J. (2013). Between water and words: Reflective self-awareness and symbol formation in art therapy. *International Journal of Art Therapy 18*(3), 122–131. https://doi.org/10.1080/17454832.2013.786107

Kana, R. K., Keller, T. A., Cherkassky, V. L., Minshew, N. J., & Just, M. A. (2006). Sentence comprehension in autism: Thinking in pictures with decreased functional connectivity. *Brain 129*, 2484–2493. https://doi.org/10.1093/brain/awl164

Kanner, L. (1949). Problems of nosology and psychodynamics in early childhood autism. *American Journal of Orthopsychiatry 19*(3), 416–426. https://doi.org/10.1111/j.1939-0025.1949.tb05441.x

Kapitan, L. (2007). Will art therapy cross the digital culture divide? *Art Therapy: Journal of the American Art Therapy Association 24*(2), 50–51. https://doi.org/10.10808/07421656.2007.10129591

Kapitan, L. (2009). Introduction to the special issue on art therapy's response to techno-digital culture. *Art Therapy: Journal of the American Art Therapy Association, 26*(2), 50–51, doi:10.1080/07421656.2007.10129591.

Kapp, S. K., Steward, R., Crane, L., Elliot, D., Elphick, C., Pellicano, E., & Russel, G. (2019). 'People should be allowed to do what they like': Autistic adults' views and experiences of stimming. *Autism 23*(7), 1782–1792. https://doi.org/10.1177/1362361319829628

Kasari, C., Freeman, S., & Paparella, T. (2006). Joint attention and symbolic play in young children with autism: A randomized controlled intervention study. *Journal of Child Psychology and Psychiatry 47*(6), 611–620. https://doi.org/10.1111/j.1469-7610.2005.01567.x

Kearney, A. (2015). *Understanding applied behavior analysis: An introduction to ABA for parents, teachers, and other professionals* (2nd ed.). Jessica Kingsley Publishers.

Kearns, D. (2004). Art therapy with a child experiencing sensory difficulties. *Art Therapy: Journal of the American Art Therapy Association 21*(2), 95–101. https://doi.org/10.1080/07421656.2004.10129551

Kenney, D. T. (2014). *From id to intersubjectivity: Talking about the talking cure with master clinicians*. Routledge.

Klorer, P. G. (2009). The effects of technology overload on children: An art therapist's perspective. *Art Therapy: Journal of the American Art Therapy Association 26*(2), 80–82. https://doi.org/10.1080/07421656.2009.10129742

Koegel, R., Fredeen, R., Kim, S., Danial, J., Rubinstein, D., & Koegel, L. (2012). Using perseverative interests to improve interactions between adolescents with autism and their typical peers in school settings. *Journal of Positive Behavioral Intervention 14*(3), 133–141. https://doi.org/10.1177/1098300712437043

Koo, J., & Thomas, E. (2019). Art therapy for children with autism spectrum disorder in India. *Art Therapy: Journal of the American Art Therapy Association 36*(4). https://doi.org/10.1080/07421656.2019.1644755

Kozhevnikov, M. (2007). Cognitive styles in the context of modern psychology: Toward an integrated framework of cognitive style. *Psychological Bulletin 133*, 464–481. https://doi.org/10.1037/0033-2909.133.3.464

Kozhevnikov, M., Kosslyn, S., & Shephard, J. (2005). Spatial versus object visualizers: A new characterization of visual cognitive style. *Journal of Memory and Cognition 33*, 710–726. https://doi.org/10.3758/BF03195337

Kramer, E. (1971). *Art as therapy with children*. Schocken Books.

Kramer, E. (2000). The art therapist's third hand: Reflections on art, art therapy and society at large. In E. Kramer (ed.), *Art as therapy: Collected papers* (pp.47–70). Jessica Kingsley Publishers.

Kramer, E., Williams, K., Henley, D., & Gerity, L. (1997). Art, art therapy, and the seductive environment. *American Journal of Art Therapy 35*(4), 106–117.

Kreslins, A., Robertson, A. E., & Melville, C. (2015). The effectiveness of psychosocial interventions for anxiety in children and adolescents with autism spectrum disorder: A systematic review and meta-analysis. *Child and Adolescent Psychiatry and Mental Health 9*(22), 1–12. https://doi.org/10.1186/s13034-015-0054-7

Kuo, N., & Plavnick, J. B. (2015). Using an antecedent art intervention to improve the behavior of a child with autism. *Art Therapy: Journal of the American Art Therapy Association 32*(2), 13–19. https://doi.org/10.1080/07421656.2015.1028312

Lang, R., Regester, A., Lauderdale, S., Ashbaugh, K., & Haring, A. (2010). Treatment of anxiety in autism spectrum disorders using cognitive behaviour therapy: A systemic review. *Developmental Neurorehabilitation 13*(1), 53–63. https://doi.org/10.3109/17518420903236288

Liebowitz, C. (2016, March 4). Here's what neurodiversity is—and what it means for feminism. *Everyday Feminism*. http://everydayfeminism.com/2016/03/neurodiversity-101

Liss, M., Sauliner, C., Fein, D., & Kinsbourne, M. (2006). Sensory and attention abnormalities in autistic spectrum disorders. *Autism 10*, 155–172.

Lovaas, O. I. (1987). Behavioral treatment and normal educational and intellectual functioning in young autistic children. *Journal of Consulting and Clinical Psychology* 55, 3–9.

Lovaas Institute (2018). Who is it most suitable for? www.lovaas.com/approach-suitable.php

Mahler, M. S., & Furer, M. (1968). *On human symbiosis and the vicissitudes of individuation: I. Infantile psychosis*. International Universities Press.

Mahler, M., Pine, F., & Bergman, A. (1975). *The psychological birth of the human infant*. Basic Books.

Martin, N. (2008). Assessing portrait drawings created by children and adolescents with autism spectrum disorder. *Art Therapy: Journal of the American Art Therapy Association* 25(1), 15–23. https://doi.org/10.1080/07421656.2008.10129348

Martin, N. (2009). *Art as an early intervention tool for children with autism*. Jessica Kingsley Publishers.

McKenzie, R., & Dallos, R. (2017). Autism and attachment difficulties: Overlap of symptoms, implications and innovative solutions. *Clinical Child Psychology and Psychiatry* 22(4), 632–648. https://doi.org/10.1177/1359104517707323

Milton, D. (2012). On the ontological status of autism: the "double empathy problem". *Disability and Society* 27(6), 883–887. https://doi.org/10.1080/09687599.2012.710008

Moon, B. L. (1999). The tears make me paint: The role of responsive art-making in adolescent art therapy. *Art Therapy: Journal of the American Art Therapy Association* 16(2), 78–82.

Moon, B. L. (2007). *The role of metaphor in art therapy: Theory, method, and experience*. Charles C. Thomas.

Ne'eman, A. (2012, December 7). ASAN letter on NDAA amendment. https://autisticadvocacy.org/2012/12/asan-letter-on-ndaa-amendment

Okuda, M., Okuda, D., & Mirek, D. (1999). Prime directive. In M. Okuda, D. Okuda, & D. Mirek (eds), *The Star Trek encyclopedia: A reference guide to the future*. Simon & Schuster Pocket Books.

Orr, P. P. (2005). Technology media: An exploration for "inherent qualities." *The Arts in Psychotherapy* 32, 1–11.

Orr, P. P. (2010). Social remixing: Art therapy in the digital age. In C. H. Moon (ed.), *Materials and media in art therapy* (pp.89–100). Routledge.

Orr, P. P. (2012). Technology use in art therapy practice: 2004 and 2011 comparison. *The Arts in Psychotherapy 39*, 234–238. https://doi.org/10.1016/j.aip.2012.03.010

Orr, P. P. (2016). Art therapy and digital media. In D. Gussak & M. Rosal (eds), *The Wiley handbook of art therapy* (pp.188–198). Wiley Blackwell.

Overley, L. C., Snow, M. S., Mossing, S. L., Degges-White, S., & Holmes, K. P. (2018). Exploring the experiences of play therapists working with children diagnosed with autism. *International Journal of Play Therapy 27*(1), 14–24. https://doi.org/10.1037/pla0000059

Parker-Bell, B. (1999). Embracing a future with computers and art therapy. *Art Therapy: Journal of the American Art Therapy Association 16*(4), 180–185. https://doi.org/10.1080/07421656.1999.10129482

Pollak, R. (1997). *The creation of Dr B: A biography of Bruno Bettelheim*. Simon & Schuster.

Potash, J. S. (2009). Fast food art, talk show therapy: The impact of mass media on adolescent art therapy. *Art Therapy 26*(2), 52–57. https://doi.org.10.1080/07421656.2009.10129746

Prensky, M. (2001). Digital natives, digital immigrants. *On the Horizon 9*(5), 1–6. https://doi.org/10.1108/10748120110424816

Raulston, T. J., & Machalicek, W. (2017). Early intervention for repetitive behavior in autism spectrum disorder: A conceptual model. *Journal of Developmental and Physical Disabilities 30*(1), 89–109, https://doi:10.1007/978-3-030-66445-9_13.

Regev, D., & Snir, S. (2013). Art therapy for treating children with autism spectrum disorders (ASD): The unique contribution of art materials. *Academic Journal of Creative Art Therapies 3*(2), 251–260.

Richard, D. A., More, W., & Joy, S. P. (2015). Recognizing emotions: Testing an intervention for children with autism spectrum disorders. *Art Therapy: Journal of the American Art Therapy Association 32*(1), 13–19. https://doi.org/10.1080/07421656.2014.994163

Roberts, J. (2021). Nothing about social skills training is neurodivergence-affirming—Absolutely nothing. [Blog post]. *Therapist Neurodiversity Collective*. https://therapistndc.org/nothing-about-social-skills-training-is-neurodivergence-affirming

Robison, J. E. (2013, October 7). What is neurodiversity? *Psychology Today*. www.psychologytoday.com/us/blog/my-life-aspergers/201310/what-is-neurodiversity

Rory's Story Cubes (2021). www.storycubes.com/en

Salter, K., Beamish, W., & Davies, M. (2016). The effects of child-centered play therapy (CCPT) on the social and emotional growth of young Australian children with autism. *International Journey of Play Therapy 25*(2), 78–90, doi:10.1037/pla0000012.

Salter Ainsworth, M. D. (1969). Object relations, dependency and attachment: A theoretical review of the infant–mother relationship. *Child Development 40*, 969–1025. https://doi.org/10.2307/1127008

Salter Ainsworth, M. D. (1989). Attachments beyond infancy. *American Psychologist 44*, 709–716. https://doi.org/10.1037/0003-066X.44.4.709

Salter Ainsworth, M. D., Blehar, M. C., Waters, M. C., & Wall, S. (1978). *Patterns of attachment*. Lawrence Erlbaum.

Schermer, V. L. (2000). Contributions of object relations theory and self psychology to relational psychology and group psychotherapy. *International Journal of Group Psychotherapy 50*(2), 199–217. https://doi.org/10.1080/00207284.2000.11490998

Schopler, E., Reichler, R. J., & Renner, B. R. (1988). Childhood Autism Rating Scale. Western Psychological Services.

Schweizer, C. (1997). Boundaries provide space: Structuring in art therapy. *Tijdschrift Voor Creatieve Therapie 27*(1), 14–18.

Schweizer, C., Knorth, E. J., & Spreen, M. (2014). Art therapy with children with autism spectrum disorders: A review of clinical case descriptions on "what works." *The Arts in Psychotherapy 41*(5), 577–593. https://doi.org/10.1016/j.aip.2014.10.009

Schweizer, C., Spreen, M., & Knorth, E. J. (2017). Exploring what works in art therapy with children with autism: Tacit knowledge of art therapists. *Art Therapy: Journal of the American Art Therapy Association 34*(4), 183–191. https://doi.org/10.1080/07421656.2017.1392760

Schweizer, C., Knorth, E. J., Spreen, M., vanYperen, T.A., & Spreen, M. (2020). Evaluation of "Image of Self," an art therapy program for children diagnosed with autism spectrum disorders (ASD). *Children and Youth Services Review 116*. https://doi.org/10.1016/j.childyouth.2020.105207

Selfe, L. (1977). *Nadia: A case of extraordinary drawing ability in an autistic child*. Academic Press.

Silberman, S. (2015). *Neurotribes: The legacy of autism and the future of neurodiversity*. Avery.

Slade, A. (2009). Mentalizing the unmentalizable: Parenting children on the spectrum. *Journal of Infant, Child, and Adolescent Psychotherapy 8*, 7–21. https://doi.org/10.1080/15289160802683054

Small, G. W., Moody, T. D., Siddarth, P., & Bookheimer, S. Y. (2009). Your brain on Google: Patterns of cerebral activation during Internet searching. *American Journal of Geriatric Psychiatry 17*(2), 116–126. https://doi.org/10.1097/JGP.0b013e3181953a02

Springham, N., & Huet, V. (2018). Art as relational encounter: An ostensive communication theory of art therapy. *Art Therapy: Journal of the American Art Therapy Association 35*(1), 4–10. https://doi.org/10.1080/07421656.2018.1460103

Stolorow, R. D., & Atwood, G. E. (1996). The intersubjective perspective. *The Psychoanalytic Review 83*(2), 181–194.

Strevett-Smith, A. (2010). Dramatherapy in the context of systemic family therapy: Towards systemic dramatherapy. *Dramatherapy 32*(1), 8–13. https://doi.org/10.1080/21571430.2010.11675762

Suskind, R. (2014). *Life animated: A story of sidekicks, heroes and autism.* Kingswell.

Sze, K. M.-F., & Wood, J. J. (2007). Cognitive behavioral treatment of comorbid anxiety disorders and social difficulties in children with high-functioning autism: A case report. *Journal of Contemporary Psychotherapy 37*, 133–143. https://doi.org/10.1007/s10879-007-9048-y

Thong, S. A. (2007). Redefining the tools of art therapy. *Art Therapy: Journal of the American Art Therapy Association 24*(2), 52–58. https://doi.org/10.1080/07421656.2007.10129583

Vandewater, E. A., Rideout, V. J., Wartella, E. A., Huang, X., Lee, J. H., & Shim, M. (2006). Digital childhood: Electronic media and technology use among infants, toddlers and preschoolers. *Pediatrics 119*(5), e1006–e1015. https://doi.org/10.1542/peds.2006-1804

Van Lith, T., Stallings, J. W., & Harris, C. E. (2017). Discovering good practice for art therapy with children who have autism spectrum disorder. *The Arts in Psychotherapy 54*, 78–84. https://doi.org/10.1016/j.aip.2017.01.002

Van Lith, T., Stallings, J., Harris, C., & Campbell, M. (2017). Practitioner survey: Developing evidence-based practice for working with individuals with autism. Paper presented at the Annual Conference of the American Art Therapy Association, November, Albuquerque, NM.

Vismara, L. A., & Lyons, G. L. (2007). Using perseverative interests to elicit joint attention behaviors in young children with autism: Theoretical and clinical implications for understanding motivation. *Journal of Positive Behavior Interventions 9*(4), 214–228. https://doi.org/10.1177/10983007070090040401

Walker, N. (2021). Neurodiversity: Some basic terms and definitions. *Neuroqueer*. https://neuroqueer.com/neurodiversity-terms-and-definitions

Williams, R. R. (Prod. & Dir.) (2016). *Life Animated: A Story of Sidekicks, Heroes and Autism* [Motion picture]. A&E Indie Films.

Winnicott, D. W. (1971). *Playing and reality*. Routledge.

Wolf Bordonaro, G., Stallings, J., & Humburg, K. (2017). Partnering Royals charities and art therapy: Grant funded arts and autism programming. Poster session presented at the Annual Conference of the American Art Therapy Association, November, Albuquerque, NM.

Subject Index

Author Index

Getting On in the Creative Arts Therapies

A Hands-On Guide to Personal and Professional Development

Erin Partridge
Foreword by Carolyn Brown Treadon

£17.99 | $24.95 | PB | 192pp |

ISBN 978 1 78775 263 4 | eISBN 978 1 78775 264 1

What do you really want from your career, and how are you going to get it? How do you find the right people and make the right connections along the way? What are the secrets of finding fulfilment in your work?

This book is intended to help you to answer these questions—and many more. Written to inspire and motivate you as you progress through your career as a creative arts therapist, it shares diverse stories and experiences spanning different career paths and decisions. The book also tackles common early career challenges including designing services, advocacy and collaborative working, exploring how adverse circumstances can be used as opportunities for growth.

With creative and reflective exercises throughout to help you to identify your goals and achieve them, this book is an indispensable guide for any creative arts therapist who wants to flourish in their career.

What I Want to Talk About

How Autistic Special Interests Shape a Life

Pete Wharmby

£13.99 | $19.95 | PB | 224pp |

ISBN 978 1 78775 827 8 | eISBN 978 1 78775 828 5

"This book isn't a memoir. It is a love letter to the phenomenon of autistic hyper-fixation."

In *What I Want to Talk About* popular autism advocate Pete Wharmby takes readers on a journey through his special interests, illuminating the challenges of autistic experience along the way. Funny, revealing, celebratory and powerful in equal measure, this is a book that will resonate with many, and which should be required reading for anyone who wants to understand autism with more accuracy and empathy.

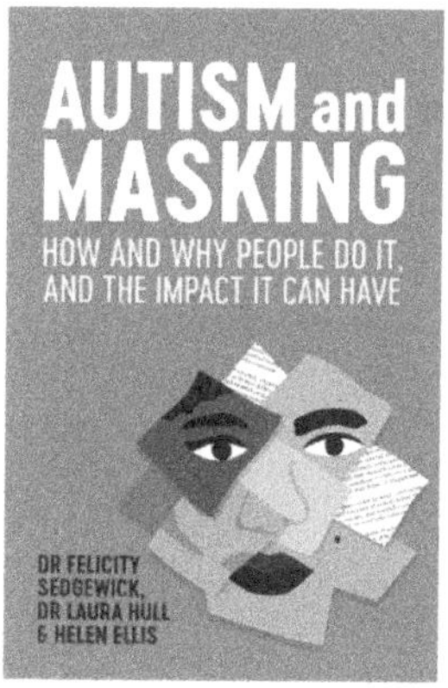

Autism and Masking

How and Why People Do It, and the Impact It Can Have

Dr Felicity Sedgewick, Dr Laura Hull and Helen Ellis

£16.99 | $24.95 | PB | 272pp |

ISBN 978 1 78775 579 6 | eISBN 978 1 78775 580 2

Autistic people often feel they have to present as neurotypical or perform neurotypical social behaviours in order to fit in. So-called "masking" is a social survival strategy used by autistic people in situations where neurodiversity is not understood or welcomed. While this is a commonly observed phenomenon in the autistic community, the complexities of masking are still not widely understood.

This book combines the latest research with personal case studies detailing autistic experiences of masking. It explains what masking is and the various strategies used to mask in social situations. The research also delves into the psychology behind masking and the specifics of masking at school, at social events with peers, and at work. The book looks at the consequences of masking, including the toll it can have on mental and physical health, and suggests guidance for family, professionals, and employers to ameliorate negative effects.

With a diverse range of voices, including perspectives across gender, ethnicity and age, this is the comprehensive guide to masking and how to support autistic people who mask.

A Graphic Guide to Art Therapy

Amy Huxtable with Gaelynn P. Wolf Bordonaro and Libby Schmanke

£16.99 | $22.95 | PB | 288pp |

ISBN 978 1 78775 351 8 | eISBN 978 1 78775 352 5

What are the core concepts of art therapy? What can you learn from a drawing of a bird's nest, a collage or some scribbles? Why become an art therapist and how do you do it? What happens in the therapy room?

In the style of a graphic novel, *A Graphic Guide to Art Therapy* answers these questions and more. Art therapy and its key concepts, theory and practice are introduced through illustrations and text. Beginning with an overview of art therapy as both a practice and a career, it shows the routes to becoming an art therapist and what the role entails. The essential approaches, frameworks, techniques and assessment styles of art therapy are visualised and discussed, making this book the perfect companion on your journey as an art therapist.

Therapeutic Adventures with Autistic Children

Connecting through Movement, Play and Creativity

Jonas Torrance

£15.99 | $26.95 | PB | 176pp |

ISBN 978 1 78592 455 2 | eISBN 978 1 78450 831 9

A vivid exploration of working with autistic children using empowering techniques from a range of creative therapies. Each chapter in this heartening book is the story of a child with autism and how therapy was pivotal in confronting his or her individual dilemma.

Covering many of the behaviours characteristic to autism, such as uncontrolled anger and obsessive tendencies, the therapies used range from drawing and dancing to meditation and martial arts, depending on the needs and interests of each child. The key message is that investing in the relationship between the therapist and the child—so that they grow, play and develop together - is transformative.